BEYOND SURVIVAL:

A Business Owner's
Guide For Success

BEYOND SURVIVAL:

A Business Owner's
Guide For Success

Léon A. Danco, Ph. D.

THE CENTER FOR FAMILY BUSINESS

university press, inc.

Post Office Box 24268
Cleveland, Ohio 44124

Library of Congress Cataloging in Publication Data

Danco, Léon A   1923-
  Beyond survival.

  1. Family corporations. 2. Small business—
Management. 3. Succession I. Title.
HD2731.D35   658'.022   74-29583
ISBN 0-9603614-0-5

© 1975, 1977, 1980, 1982 by Léon A. Danco

First Edition Published January, 1975
Reston Publishing Co., Inc.
A Prentice-Hall Company

Twelfth Printing

Printed in the
United States
of America

ACKNOWLEDGEMENT

Writing any book is like raising a child. It represents all the hopes and the dreams as well as all the anxieties, frustrations, and doubts of all creative acts. Without the encouragement and commitment of two people over a period of many years, this book would never have come into being.

Preceding even the fledgling origins of my seminars for the business owner back in the early 60's in the basement of the library at John Carroll University, Dr. Arthur J. Noetzel, former Dean of the School of Business and now Vice President for Academic Affairs at the University, has made himself ever available to me for counsel and support as both teacher and friend. I am truly indebted to him for his contributions—too numerous to mention—to the creation of these seminars which over the years have brought me into contact with the many thousands of business owners whom I have come to know and respect.

Over an even longer period of time, the love and understanding of my wife, Katy, has provided a constant tenderness which never wavered during the many years that I have sought to serve the business community. I am grateful beyond expression for her recognition and acceptance of the price that must be paid by all of us—the lonely days, the sleepless nights, the risks taken, and the battles lost—for the victories we have shared. She has given to me whatever understanding I may now have.

Léon A. Danco

"In His wisdom God gives to each of us a limited, finite number of hours a year in which to achieve our goals, both material and spiritual. He gives us these hours in sequence, day by day, month by month. If they are wasted, however, they are neither repeatable nor refundable. He gives the same amount to the rich and to the poor, to the young and to the old. Whatever successes we may achieve in this life will come from the purpose to which we put God's priceless gift — *time*."

Léon A. Danco, Ph.D.

PREFACE

The person who founds a business is usually equated to and given a form of respect reserved only for mothers, Marine Corps sergeants, wealthy baseball players, and federal judges. They have become sacred cows. No one ever says anything mean about these people. They are called the bulwark of our American way of life. To be against them would be un-American. And the bigger their business, the bigger their halo.

The admiration and respect accorded these owner presidents assures their position within their community. They are considered the educational leaders, the financial leaders, and the civic leaders of their town. And the smaller the community, the bigger their personal stature. Great demand is made on the time of a successful owner president. He has to be good. He has to be tremendous. I am not sure at what, but he has to be good. Everyone says so.

Back in Hometown, U.S.A., the owner president of a family company is likened unto God. The bank needs his deposits; the town needs his payroll; every civic and community activity needs his blessing. His suppliers like his business, and his employees know they haven't got another job, if they get thrown out. It is very easy for him to confuse power with divinity.

In addition to holding a respected position in society, the owner of a family business has other and not-so-worthy, characteristics—long-term incumbency, secrecy, dummy boards of directors, and the innate problems of his company's limited size—limited funds, limited time, and limited opportunities. These latter are *real* limits, but they are by far the minor limits on his activity. His real problems are that:

1. He has been at it too long,

2. His experience is invalid,

3. He does not tell anyone anything,

4. He does not want other people to meddle in his affairs,

5. He is influenced by a corps of co-conspirators masquerading as advisors and sometimes as directors.

As a teacher, advisor and consultant to many closely held businesses, I am convinced that the privately held company is an endangered species. The threat lies not so much from competitors, regulatory legislation, consumer movements or other outside forces. The real threat to the private business lies primarily within the business practices and policies of its owners. Too many family owned companies seem to suffer from "corporeuthanasia," a term I like to use to describe the owner's act of willfully killing off the business he loves by failing to provide in his lifetime for a viable organization with clear continuity. This disaster occurs because the owner of the business cannot face the fact that at some point he must . . . and will be replaced. If the successful business owner, who had the ability, vision, and guts to build his business from nothing, does not have the courage to face the problems of the future, then his banker and attorney will do it for him on the way back from his funeral—four cars back from the flowers.

Léon A. Danco

CONTENTS

Chapter One

Introduction

Powerful is the best description for a successful business owner of a family held business. He has a power equaled only by the wartime captain of ships at sea, and tenured full professors in their classrooms. The owner president is both the creator and beneficiary of his own power, a power maintained by secrecy and non-review.

Although the successful business owner enjoys the many fruits of his labor, he has become confused by the sudden acquisition of this power. It has provided him with unaccustomed and unprecedented privilege. With this privilege have come both responsibility and fear; responsibility for fulfilling some of the expectations his power has elicited from others, and fear that it may all disappear before he has really enjoyed it.

The smaller the world in which his business exists, the more powerful, usually, is the owner president. He can pontificate with impunity on anything from the rise of the mini-skirt to the decline of the priesthood. He has become a power unto himself, and after awhile, his power is transformed into Divinity. He begins to feel that

1

he is immortal, that he will never need to relinquish this omnipotence, and that he will never die.

But, in fact, he must make a very mortal decision. At some point, he must decide to provide the mechanism for the profitable growth and continuity of his business after he's gone, or, he will destroy on his way down, what he's built on his way up. The very qualities which made him powerful and helped to create the independence and prestige he treasures, secrecy and lack of outside review, carry within them the seeds of destruction to his company.

This book is intended to examine this man and the world he has built around himself, to peel it apart as an onion, and look at him, his world and his growth and development, layer by layer. Only in this way can we overcome the opaque nature of his secrecy and discover his true nature; a lonely man who is harassed, confused, tired, secretive, non-reviewed, disorganized, evasive, parochial, pedestrian, insular, successful, powerful and scared.

Let us explore together this world of the business owner—a great man with all the qualities both good and bad that make us human beings. Let us try to provide him with a mirror in which to see himself and the development of his business as he has lived it but rarely reflected upon it.

Let us concern ourselves, however, with the life of the business winners, not the losers; with the normal, not the neurotic; with the honest and hardworking, not with the scroungers and the chiselers and the cheaters. For these others, the book will have no meaning.

But for those who find the need in the prime of their life to reexamine the bittersweet taste of success, to reflect on their reactions to it, and to take this opportunity for second thoughts and, perhaps, a second chance, this book is about them, their lives, their work, their fears and their dreams.

This book results from the dedication of a lifetime of work within the world of the business owner as participant, observer, teacher, writer, and friend. I hope I can repay the understanding shared with me by the many thousands of business owners (and their families and associates) whom I have come to know so well in the course of my lectures, consultations, and seminars.

For some time I have sensed among business owners an increasing need for a better understanding of where they have been and where they are going. This is not an instructional guide for starting a business. Rather, it is for the established entrepreneur who must face eventually the problem of perpetuating a successful business beyond his own time. It is my hope that this book will help to affirm for the business owner his unique identity and prompt him into some positive actions to solve those problems he has avoided too long or whose existence he has denied.

But don't take my thoughts out of context. No one sentence is meant to stand alone. Some statements are really questions; some ideas are meant to make you mad; some thoughts are stated in reverse. Mostly, I talk, not write. The subtle inferences which I can make by intonation, gesture, and emotion in speaking are difficult to transcribe on paper. My metaphors are mixed; my analogies may be bad; I may be accused of exaggeration; but I want to be understood and judged by the whole of my thought, not by its pieces.

This book is written for the business owner in an attempt to present a mature view of his life as he has lived it and is now living it. As a man ages, he begins to reflect upon his past, upon what he has done, his values change, his view of success changes. He needs to integrate the separate patterns of his life—to see himself as a whole man; part owner, part manager, part worker, and part father hus band.

He needs to accept

(1) an objective perspective on the crucial problems of management succession on the future of his business; and

(2) some insight into the alternatives available to him for the preservation and continuity of his assets and his goals within the family company.

If the owner manager is able to see himself in this story, then there can be hope for the survival of his creation. If I can define and identify him and his work so that we can understand each other, then, hopefully, we can work together on some alternative solutions and the actions needed to implement them.

This book is also written for the business owner's wife whose counsel and loving care provided the support so necessary for her husband over the years he built his company. Hopefully it will provide her with

(1)   a clearer understanding of her husband's business, its problems and opportunities,

(2)   some insights into the necessary differences between personal or family goals, and company objectives, and how to reconcile them, and

(3)   some clues, perhaps, how she can best lend support to her husband now as he struggles with the greater complexities of today's world.

To the heirs and successors of owner managers, the young who are affected by or will affect the business, to the young who will someday inherit the family business for better or for worse—this book is also addressed. By understanding the struggles and dreams of the founders of the business, they may be able to understand why the man who built this business for them finds it so hard to turn it over to them and leave it. And they may be able to help him—and themselves.

THE PROSPECTS FOR SURVIVAL

If you are kidding yourself about the nature of a family held company and its innate problems you are preparing to add one more statistic to the business mortality figures in this country. Failure to provide for the perpetuity of your business beyond your working lifetime means simply that you have overstated your profits, for when you go, the whole company goes with you.

As a teacher, advisor and consultant to many closely held businesses, I am convinced that the privately held company is an endangered species. The threat lies not so much from competitors, regulatory legislation, consumer movements or other outside forces. The real threat to the private business lies primarily within the business practices and policies of its owners. Too many family owned companies seem to suffer from "corporeuthanasia," a term I use to describe the owner's act of willfully killing off the business he loves by failing to provide in his lifetime for a viable organization with clear continuity. This disaster occurs because the owner of the business cannot face the fact that at some point he must . . . and will be replaced. If the successful business owner, who had the ability, vision and guts to build his business from nothing, does not have the courage to face the problems of the future, then his banker and attorney will do it for him on the way back from his funeral—four cars back from the flowers.

These may sound like harsh words, but I have witnessed the destruction of too many worthwhile family businesses in the last years of the founder's life to sit idly by and watch the entrepreneurial sector expire when I know that its illnesses are curable. I have great faith in the value of the privately owned business and the need for its survival and growth. To conceive one's own business, to toil in one's own vineyard, to enjoy the fruits of one's own labor, and to be able to pass on the creation of one's own hand to a chosen successor is to share in the work of our Creator and to help assure the fulfillment of His promise in our own time and in our own world.

The family owned business is the strength of America. In each time of crisis, the business owner has come through a winner while others wring their hands and whine. Business owners as a whole know what it takes to come out ahead. They have scratched their way up a splintery ladder to success. The problem is that when they finally reach the top, they look around from their current position of power and success and they wonder what it is they are supposed to do next. If new answers are not readily forthcoming, they repeat what they did before. Therein lies the problem.

At some point the business owner must recognize that success has radically changed his relationship to his company. He must understand that businesses which survive do so because the founder has taken measures to assure the continuity of his company. Unless he is willing to have his business close up when he is through playing with it—in which case he doesn't really have a business but a profitable hobby—the business owner must change his role from that of super employee to that of respected leader and teacher, who must gain his ultimate glory in the accomplishments of those who follow him.

How does the average business owner manage this transformation? Too few founders or inheritors know how to seek help or even what aid they need to make this transition. The kind of help that busy company presidents require is not readily available from conventional educational sources, which are geared to providing assistance to professional managers in the publicly owned corporation. The family held business is hostile territory, and the owners are too often unwilling or unable to share their fears and concerns with those who could help them.

SOME HOPELESS CASES

In the past year, I have declined invitations to do some consulting work for three separate companies totalling over $50 million in sales. Neglect has created a terminal situation in each case. They have had it, but won't understand or accept it. There are some 1600 employees involved in these companies who will be on the street in short order. I did not accept the assignments because I do not work on hopeless cases.

In one case a substantial construction company is going to go down the drain. Dad, now in his late 60's, is still putting in a 10 hour day at the office, 6-7 days a week. His two sons, 43 and 39, have worked for Dad for 22 and 17 years respectively. Yet, after two decades of full-time, in-company "experience," neither has learned how to deal with errors in judgment because neither has had the right to make any. Neither has ever been consulted on major policies or decisions of the company. Neither has ever been given any meaningful responsibility. Dad has called every shot. In their feeling of emasculation, the younger son drinks like a draft dodger, and the elder is separated from his second wife. Now, at a time when old Dad thinks he would finally like to step down, he is too afraid or ashamed to turn over his business to his sons whom he has destroyed. But he's worth $2½ million on the books.

In another case, a 30 year old specialty rubber manufacturing company is owned by three brothers who each recently inherited 1/3 of the common stock at Dad's death. The older sons had entered the company immediately following college and have "worked their way up" in the organization. The third brother went to work for a major supplier for about 10 successful years and then asked Dad if he could come back and use *his* experience in the family concern. As an outsider he looked at the operation with an objectivity unappreciated either by Dad or his brothers. He predicted a dangerous business decline unless the company reorganized several phases of its manufacturing and marketing program. He also suggested some changes in the accounting system to provide more information to all managers, family or not.

Unfortunately, the two brothers who had been plowing the family furrows for those ten years felt that the third brother who had been working "outside" was abrasive, inexperienced and didn't understand their business. Fights resulted in his quitting and going back to work for his old company. The brothers continued to run the firm their way. Shortages of vital materials and the loss of major markets to aggressive competitors have generated such severe losses for the last two years that insolvency is now only a matter of time. With the company facing collapse, it doesn't help the business now for the third brother to say, "I told you so." His third isn't worth much, now, and nor are his brothers' shares. Mother and the family lawyer both told me recently that the older boys never did like to take advice. Too bad. They'll be taking orders from now on.

Finally, in a third case, that of a prominent industrial distributorship, the founder died several years ago leaving his widow as president and chief executive officer of the company. In actual fact, she spends only about four days a month in the office posting payables to justify her compensation to the IRS. Although her name is on the letterhead, the company is actually run by the collusion of the former general manager and vice president of sales, the attorney who drew up the trust agreements, and the outside accountant who has been with the company since it was founded. Collectively they keep the widow ignorant of operations. She doesn't dare protest for she doesn't understand enough to interfere with their decisions.

The company is being both milked and destroyed by the hangers-on who keep the widow's only son on the road as "a sales manager" under the excuse that low profits will not permit hiring more outside help. Mother is frightened that the business will not support her old age, and the son is beginning the realize that when he finally succeeds to his inheritance, there will be nothing to inherit. The plight of this family could have been avoided had Dad planned for his succession and rid himself of the piranhas around him while he was still alive and in charge. I remember him from earlier seminars when he said he was going to clean out the deadwood. Now it is too late for me to undo the damage his lack of decision has perpetrated. It's hard to buck a self-seeking, self-perpetuating voting trust.

I wish I could say that these cases are unusual. Unfortunately, they are not. Similar situations occur all too frequently in family owned companies. My fear is that unless more business owners take steps to change their essential management practices, the privately owned company could virtually disappear in one generation. The irony is that their great success threatens their survival.

THE DANGERS OF SUCCESS

For the past decade, the entrepreneur has been riding a crest of economic success. Used to a lean, hungry, financial status, he suddenly discovered he was affluent, powerful, and able to buy almost whatever he wished. He grew fat and overconfident. During the '60's and early '70's, most of my speeches were a sobering intervention into this self-satisfied world. I attempted to point out to this business owner that he could not afford to rest on his laurels, to coast at the comfort level. He needed to share his business dreams and skills with those who would follow after him.

My remarks were made in the context of a self-indulgent world. We had plenty. We were enjoying the highest standard of living in the world. We had reinvented Babylon. Many of the ideas advanced in this book were originally developed during that period. Now we are faced with an Armageddon and, as an entire nation, are experiencing a changing lifestyle. The dawn of a new struggle, the struggle to maintain and bolster our sagging resources has increased the urgency for the owner of a family business to put his house in order.

The business owner is lonely, tired, scared, harassed and confused. The energy crisis, the environmental crises, the increase of government regulation and economic policy by edict have served only to heighten that confusion. More than ever before, the business owner needs help from trusted, competent advisors; help from a sound board of directors. He needs both a plan and an organization for carrying on the business; a management team that realizes the full effects of their decisions, a family which understands his dream, and successors in whom he can have confidence. As the climate in which he operates becomes more stringent and, perhaps, more oppressive, those qualities which often have worked against him, his smallness, his lack of momentum, his narrow specialization, and his insulation, may be in fact, the very qualities which can help assure his survival.

Whatever he chooses to do with his business, he cannot continue to run it only to provide bigger and better comforts. Conditions beyond his control have today eliminated many of those comforts. The business owner is caught up in a new kind of struggle. At stake is the survival of a way of life which he cherishes. Unlike previous business skirmishes during the building of the business, these crises find the owner at the top of his growth cycle. He must make a decision. Is his business going to continue to grow, or has he wearied of the struggle? Can he turn it over to someone else? How? Who cares? For the first time, perhaps, the legends that he has woven into his personal history—his memories of "The Depression," or of the period he recalls as "The War"—may be shared and understood by his successors through the kind of comradeship and cooperation this new struggle requires.

In order to understand the alternatives in his future, the business owner must understand where he has been and how he has reached this present position. When he can see himself moving through time, headed into a future which he himself helps call into being, then he can understand and share in the excitement and challenge that lies ahead. But, before he can talk about his future, he must accept and understand his past and use it as the cornerstone of his new accomplishments.

That the family owned business will survive and grow, I am confident. One of the major qualities of the business owner is his courage. He works best when the chips are down, when the tide is rising, and the alligators swarm around his ankles. It is affluence which causes him trouble, for he does not know what he is supposed to do with it. The business owner is a fighter. Give him a good scrap and he will come out ahead. He has the flexibility to change and adapt, if change and adaptation are the ingredients of survival. He is small enough to remain lean and hungry and still not starve. He can ride out a storm until better times arrive. And he has a confidence born of battles fought and won. He may not like to relive some of the hard times, but he knows that he can do it and survive. This time around, he need not be alone. He needs to recognize his heirs, and his successors, who must be with him to learn and to share in his struggle as his junior officers, and who must, themselves, in due time take over his command. Though many may face the radical changes of the future with fear, the business owner should face them with hope. He has the ability and the guts to win. And, by his example, to lead.

Chapter Two

Where is the Entrepreneur?

In the United States there are roughly 210 million people. Of these, about 90 million people work, although "working" is defined in various ways. They work in 11 million institutions: U.S. Steel, The Split Lip Manufacturing Company, Inc., an independent farm, the XYZ Supply Company, Standard Oil, or a book store, any unit in which people can be employed. Since every unit has a "boss," one man out of eight works for himself with or without other employees. Of these 11 million institutions, 10 million are partnerships and proprietorships: small stores, farmers on 10 acres, contractors with one truck, manufacturer's agents, and dentists. In terms of the number of economic units, they are the largest group of all. As measured by the Gross National Product, however, the largest percentage of American business activity is done in the corporate form.

There are over a million corporations in the United States, but these corporations are not all alike. They include General Motors at the top of the scale and an incorporated car wash at the bottom.

Of these 1 million corporations, the so-called "big board" companies—those listed on the New York, American, and Regional Exchanges and closely regulated by the Securities and Exchange Commission—number only about 5000. Of these the Fortune 500 List, the Forbes List, and Dun's Review List, make note of perhaps 1000 of the biggest.

In addition, there is the so-called "over the counter" market, those regional companies and smaller corporations whose stocks do not enjoy national interest. This listing includes such companies as local banks, local utility companies, and local suppliers of goods and services. The "over the counter" companies number about 20,000 companies. When companies "go public" they are added to this list. When they are bought up by bigger companies, they are removed. And the net number increases about a thousand a year.

The total number of companies in which part ownership can be purchased on the open market is, therefore, not much more than 25,000. Out of a million corporations in this country, only 25,000 are publicly owned, that is 2½%. Of these the largest is General Motors with an annual sales volume in excess of thirty billion dollars. The number of corporations with an annual sales volume in excess of $200 million is only 1000. That is only 4% of all the publicly owned corporations and only 1/10 of 1% of the total number of corporations in the nation.

Employee census indicates that only 50,000 corporations including both publicly owned and privately held companies employ more than a hundred people and only 200,000 more companies have over 25 employees. All remaining employees work in a variety of businesses hiring from one to 25 people. When it comes to analyzing who works where and generates what, one discovers that half of the work force is employed in publicly held companies producing only one half of the GNP. The remaining work force, the other half, works in privately held companies and generates the other half of the GNP.

But these companies comprise two distinct worlds. The 25,000 companies that are public corporations with professional managers barely make a dent in the one million corporations in existence in the United States. About 97% of all companies inhabit the "world of the private business owner." Stock in these businesses is not for sale except under special circumstances. Privately held companies have very little in common with the world of "big business." All the boys at the country club bar talk about the big, well-known companies they read about, but the business owner lives in the land of the great unknown; the privately owned, family managed, closely held company.

CORPORATIONS—PUBLIC AND PRIVATE

The management policies of publicly held companies have nothing to do with the management practices of privately owned companies. The men and the motives running them are different. It's a lot like the difference between the pilot of a 707 and the bush league private flyer who uses his single engine bird to call on customers or take his family on vacation.

The same is true of the private company. The president pilots his own craft and it takes him where he wants to go. In contrast, the president of a publicly owned corporation is one of several pilots in the stockholders' airplane, and he flies it pretty much where they tell him to go. One 707 is pretty much like any other and so are their pilots.

Until a relatively few years ago all businesses in this country were privately owned, one plane and one pilot. Then along came the 707's, the corporate giants with ownership of the public company vested in a large number of unknown persons. It became necessary for those companies to create self-perpetuating organizational structures which did not depend upon specific individuals for their continuity. These structures, in turn, caused the development of mobile professional managers whose loyalty was generally to their profession and not necessarily to the company. Executive nomads, they could roam the country fitting into any public company with ease, since the organization of their new company virtually duplicated the organization from which they came.

The development of large corporations seeking managers from outside the family led to a need for special education for these managers. The growth of business schools was a means of filling this need. But business administration programs, undergraduate or graduate, were not devised to assist the private business owner. Managers of publically owned companies, like airline pilots, are professional managers, competitively selected, highly trained and highly mobile. Presidents of privately held companies are not selected on merit. They appoint themselves. They don't know nor does anyone else know, if they are doing the right thing, but they own the plane, and it hasn't crashed, yet.

Because they don't identify with him, most people don't care about the president of the privately held company or the private pilot. Despite the fact that half of our nation's employees are dependent upon him, few people understand the essential character of the family owned business; its pressures, its frustrations, its satisfactions and its promise. No wonder they are fearful. Even the business owner does not recognize that he is an endangered species, and that the essential problems of his future find their roots in the nature of his past.

Despite public opinion to the contrary, the United States is still mostly a nation of first-generation businesses. The founder of the business is generally still alive, still owner, and probably still working, because in this great country of ours, the average life expectancy of any business is only 24 years, the working lifetime of one man. It's 24 years long counting only those companies that survive the high mortality rate of business infancy in the first ten years.

Even those businesses that do survive and outgrow the hazards of start-up rarely carry over into a viable second generation after the death of the founder. Like the number of multiple marriages, the number of multiple-generation businesses is hard to quantify with any accuracy. The preponderance of the evidence available, however, highlights the regrettable fact that, in the past, most businesses which have survived their founder by several future generations, have done so only through the absorption of their assets by the publicly owned and professionally managed conglomerates. Too often only the name of the founder remains as a reminder that here lies the dream of an entrepreneur.

Whether they realize it or not, broad sectors of the people and the businesses in our United States are influenced by the privately held, family owned business. These companies account for over 95 percent of the business units in the United States, 50% of all non-governmental workers, and they generate nearly half of the gross national product.

A recent government survey indicates that privately owned businesses represent a large proportion of companies and sales volume in many fields:

(1)   in construction, 99% of all firms and 88% of all sales

(2)   in retail service or distribution, 96% of all firms and 72% of all sales

(3)   in wholesaling, 94% of all firms and 70% of all sales

(4)   in manufacturing, 94% of all firms and 30% of all sales

Similarly, in the area of philanthropy, through the gifts of the owner's time and money, the privately owned business is the chief supporter of most private schools, colleges, and universities, most community and religious charities. The business owner is the representative on the boards of directors of most of our nations' banks, hospitals, schools, and social agencies.

If the privately owned business were to disappear, it would be a socio-economic disaster to our way of life. Private business enterprise maintains the routine activities of daily living as well as business. Unlike the monolithic corporate giant whose head is lost in the clouds of its bigness, the private business is easy to locate if you only know how to recognize it.

In many of the smaller towns in America in which his business is a major industry, the business owner is, in fact, the giver of life. If his business closes its doors, the town, also, will suffer. The West does not hold a patent on ghost towns. The smaller the town, the more powerful is the business owner. People take off their hats when they talk to him on the phone. Even in the larger metropolitan areas, where his power as an individual employer may be miniscule compared with publicly owned corporations, the privately held business owner wields unusual influence. His business is the backbone of numerous established institutions. For example:

Most of the manufacturing industry in this country depends upon *distributors* to fully market or service its products. The individual distributor, 9 times out of 10, is a closely held, owner-managed business. When the distributor ceases to do business in his market area, the companies he represents are also out of business in that community. To publicly owned corporations, the distributor is a vital ingredient to their success. His power over their well being is real, but it is often unacknowledged.

In another role, the private businessman enjoys a totally different, but equally valuable, relationship *as a supplier* to the publicly held corporation. Because of its size, location, flexibility, unique resources, or specific skills, the family owned company is usually in a good position to assume the sub-contracted manufacturing or servicing of parts, products, or assemblies which are unsuitable operations for a large corporation. A significant segment of privately owned business is involved as a vital supplier of goods and services to industry at a profit to both. General Motors even advertises that it "buys" from over 20,000 "small businesses."

Looking at the owner manager as a *contractor/builder* we must realize that most of the houses we live in, the offices, the stores, and the factories we work in, the suburban centers we shop in, the highways we travel on, the bridges we cross over, the airports we land on, are designed, built, and serviced by privately held, owner-managed companies. Though the equipment and the materials may be the output of industrial giants and conglomerates, the structures didn't exist until a private entrepreneur put them all together.

AS A VITAL FORCE TO THE BUSINESS COMMUNITY AT LARGE, THE BUSINESS OWNER IS INDISPENSABLE:

• *Banks* across the nation, in many cases "family businesses" themselves, are beginning to recognize the business owner and his company as their most important customer classification. They prosper from his payroll, his payables, his loans, his trusts, and his investments. He is both the supplier and the distributor of their product, "money."

• *Life insurance companies* consider the "business owner market" as their single most profitable area of operations. They are well aware of the owner-manager's need for "security" and income in his old age, and they package their products to appeal to his feud with the IRS.

• *Stockbrokers* consider owner/managers pigeons second only to dentists. They are prime prospects for every new tip on market fluctuation or new issue as a hedge to putting all their eggs in one basket.

• *The business service professionals* such as lawyers, accountants and consultants of every description fawn on the business owner. His continuing business needs coupled with his basic concentration on product and market relationship, and his dislike for "figures," unions, government regulations of all sorts and the IRS in particular, make him the mainstay of their offices as a liable, taxable, accountable, and insurable economic mealticket. He never outlives them.

• *Non-profit organizations* both at home and abroad, are major beneficiaries of his personal good will. His philanthropy is essential to numerous charities that benefit from his suspicion of government and bigness. His individual search for immortality is a powerful stimulus for such organizations which constantly design "memorial" projects to satisfy his need to provide and survive.

And the list goes on and on. The business owner's money and his opinion have special attraction because they are not subject to review by outsiders. He acts on his "impulse" and "experience." But this can be a two-edged sword.

A BASIC DILEMMA

The privately held business is an economic structure whose growth can be limited by its management. The managers of a publicly owned corporation do not have the authority to limit the growth of their enterprise. Public shareholders demand more and more growth to provide an increasing return on investment in order to justify their continued holding of the securities. On the other hand, the privately owned distributor/supplier/customer may not want to grow. He may want only to enjoy his present level of prosperity without increased sweat, strain, or risk. Here we have a basic dilemma between the publicly owned corporation, the producer of most goods and the privately held company, the distributor/consumer of most goods.

Consider: when the 45 year old divisional sales manager of one of Fortune's 500 has to get a 20% profit increase each year to hold his job, how slowly can he let his distributor/customer "comfortably" grow? The product of his company is only *inventory* unless he can sell it. Too often, this sales manager is unable to understand and to cope with the basic problem of all manufacturer-distributor relationships: distinctly different goals and divergent views on growth. Why? The sales manager, his superiors, and his sales force are largely made up of "organization men" who still have to climb to achieve. Their function within the company is to get more products out the door this year than they did last year. Their goal is always to grow, to produce and sell more and more. They don't have much empathy with or sympathy for the problems of continuity in the privately owned distributorship, a business which they consider to be owned by an aging male or his no good kids who just want to level off and enjoy the rewards of their achievements, just keep even with the board, not sweat to increase sales nor suffer the consequences of decreased sales. The lack of perpetual go . . . go . . . go on the part of the business owner confuses the professional managers. They would rather deal with other professional managers. They understand each other. They were taught together, and they worry about the same things. It's easier for them to do business with those who inhabit worlds similar to their own. They don't know this other world of the business owner—and never did.

Unless these two sectors of business accommodate to the needs of each other with understanding and good faith, both the business world and the American public will suffer. The American economy needs both. Each exists because it provides for the other.

We, the consumers, whether we realize it or not, are the ultimate beneficiaries.

If Joe in Little City has partner problems and quits, and Bill in Podunk just liquidates in his last years, and Mike in Upper Eureka sells out because he decides his son isn't able to run the business, pretty soon the manufacturing companies they serve have a distributor network that looks pretty much like Swiss cheese. It's full of holes where the companies used to sell their product. Competitors have taken over with their own distributorships, and the publicly owned manufacturer is out of business in that territory.

Most manufacturers exist in their market only through those companies which distribute their product and the independent contractors who service their products. The private business owner is the last interface between the consumer and the public corporation in nearly every sector of human need for food, shelter, clothing and leisure at multiple levels. The loss of its distribution spells disaster to any corporation and this loss is usually fatal to the manager responsible.

In equal respect this mutual involvement and interdependence with the business owner and his company continues within all his interrelationships and with all the institutions his existence benefits. Without the creation of a continuing management beyond the aegis of the founder, there is no way that a closely held company can continue to support the corporate growth goals and share of market required of it. The greatest long term success open to a beleaguered professional sales manager is to create a continuing program in distributor management development. In fact, many major corporations are beginning to sponsor various educational seminars for their distributors for the sole purpose of keeping their own business healthy and growing.

Unfortunately, either as distributor, contractor, or supplier to the public corporation or as customer/client to the business professions, business owners too often feel trapped by the same management fear . . . a basic feeling among privately held companies that neither the big corporation nor "the professional establishment" is to be trusted. So they try to maintain an arm's length relationship with the very enterprises with whom they are essentially in partnership. They feel threatened by the slightest movement of the public corporation and its satellites in their direction, and an increasing feeling of polarization occurs.

The owner manager is an influential socio-economic entity. His money and his power represent a new establishment with its own value system. To him, his values plus his time plus his money equal "the social good." He is slowly awakening to the fact that he is no longer a second class citizen and his rallying cry is "I'm good for this country." This new awareness of his power and the responsibility which goes with it, often leaves both him and the country wondering, "Who is this business owner, and how did he get there?"

THE HERITAGE OF THE FAMILY OWNED BUSINESS

The family-owned business offers us an instant course in "ethnic studies" both Wasp and non-Wasp; the immigrant, the unemployed, the dispossessed, the uneducated. For it is within such ethnic groups that the majority of family-owned businesses in existence today had their origins over the last 50 years. Unassimilated by the Ivy League ranks of the organization man, these unappreciated men had no other means of fulfilling their ambition for power and privilege than through the sweat of their own hands and the strength of a business which they built themselves.

Because of the many different ethnic considerations of the owner of the smaller concerns, and his generally custom-tailored business practices, the private business owner seemed always to end up as the little guy . . . the underdog . . . the one who never made it in the big leagues of organized management . . . the outsider. He was always sniffing around the bush. He was always a second class manager. These were self-reinforcing qualities . . . the more the owner manager was told that he was second class, the more he believed it. It was a kind of self-fulfilling prophecy. And when he "made" it, he often blustered in his own little world, because there were others in it even more "outside" than he was.

Chapter Three

Portrait of the Business Owner

It is not only outsiders who fail to understand the nature of a closely held business and the problems of its owner. The business owner is as much an enigma to himself as he is to them. Who he is at any given moment depends as much upon who looks at him, and under what circumstances, as it does upon objective reality. His is not an identity crisis in the psychological sense. It is a crisis caused by the essential conflict between limited time and multiple roles. The symptoms of this crisis vary depending upon when the owner manager looks at himself and when others look at him in an attempt to understand him.

FOUR MEN IN ONE

In any given day, we all have 24 hours. A business owner divides this time into four parts. He has the *man* part; the human, physiological and psychological part. He has the *owner-shareholder* part. He has the *employee-worker* part, and he has the *manager -planner* part.

21

These are not perfect quarters. Everyone picks his own time use. Nobody tells the entrepreneur where to put his time. He puts some percentage into his physical-psychological needs; sleeping, eating, raising his family, relaxing, spending time with his wife and children and the rest of it is put into some form of work. If he doesn't spend this time in his work, he won't eat. He won't survive. If, as his business grows, he doesn't spend some time in policy-making, risk taking, decision-making, and long range planning, his company will not grow into the future. These conflicting roles make up the owner manager's world. (See Figure 1)

Is it any wonder, then, that the single, strong, distinguishing characteristic of this owner manager is that he's confused? He doesn't know what he's supposed to do with his time. He doesn't know what he's supposed to do with his money, his employees, his

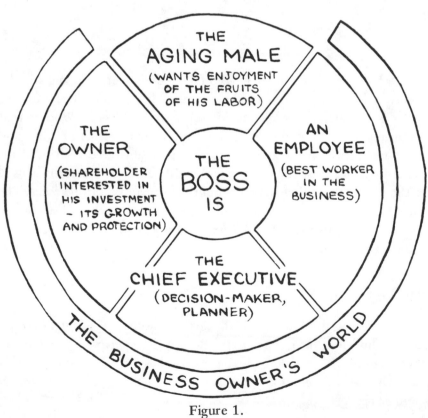

Figure 1.

business. He doesn't know whether he should buy or sell, grow or shrink; whether he should go to seminars or stay home; whether he should hang on or sell out. Poor devil, he's confused.

The reason that he is confused isn't that he's stupid, or that he doesn't understand his business field. It's that each of his roles has different requirements. If he tries to perform well in all of them, he is hopelessly swamped by conflicting claims on his attention. There is never enough time to give himself equally to all four roles. He is inexperienced in setting the priorities so that he can fulfill all of his needs in each area.

As a *shareholder* this businessman wants what any shareholder wants; R.O.I., a return on his investment. It can come as capital gain, as income, or as a mixture of the two; tax-deferred or sheltered compensation, as all sorts of things. But he wants to make money with his assets and he also wants his assets to be secure, appreciating, liquid, and useful in his old age, or he wants to convert them into other assets that will be secure—or so he hopes. Most owners who haven't "merged," secretly think that they could. Few realize that their high opinion of their "value" effectively results in nobody wanting to "acquire" them.

As the company's hardest working, most valuable *employee* he wants a job. He wants something worthwhile to do for as long as he wants to work. As *chief executive officer*, manager and planner he wants the company to grow, to "make more money," to provide increasing employment and generate more "business." As an *aging male* he wants to level off and enjoy the success and contentment he's earned but he has all sorts of problems. His hair is thinning, his arthritis is bad, his mother-in-law threatens to move in with him, and the neighbor's dog keeps digging up his prize rhododendrons; he's harassed and he's confused. He doesn't know how he got into this mess or how to get out. His problems are the problems of success.

The business owner finds himself with a successful business and an affluent life style, and the pull of his four lives becomes chaotic. If the market changes, his "investor" self prepares for alternatives; if the union threatens, his "manager" self moves in to put out that fire; if a vital machine breaks down, or a big customer complains, his "employee" self gets into the action; and if his wife reminds him that he was out of town on his last anniversary or that his daughter's birthday is tomorrow, he drops everything to fulfill himself as husband and father.

The picture any outsider has of an entrepreneur, therefore, depends upon which of these selves he has most recently encountered. Few people, including the entrepreneur, are conscious of the constant interplay, the wearying struggle between these four portions of himself. One of the ways of reconciling this confusion is to examine the typical growth pattern of an owner managed business as it is perceived by the founder, his family, and by outsiders. (See Figure 2)

THE WONDER PERIOD—THE FIRST STAGE

Most men begin their own businesses in their early thirties. Few men under thirty have acquired the self-confidence or the experience to "go it alone," and their savings or sources of credit aren't yet well enough established to get a business off the ground. Very few men over 40 have the guts or the energy to quit security and risk everything on a new venture. They don't have the extra 10 to 15 years needed to assure the rewards in time to enjoy them.

Usually a man goes into business for himself sometime in his 30's because he was fired. No one who eats regularly and sees a bright future ahead of him quits to start a business. The odds against success are too great. If he's married and has children, he's not usually willing to run the risk. So the average business owner didn't volunteer for the job. He was drafted by circumstances. He was jobless, broke, scared, and he needed to take care of his family and find work. He's a rugged individualist. He believes in the American Dream. He believes that he, himself, is the only limit to his success. Any man's grasp can exceed his reach if he will only stretch a little bit. Before his savings start to run out and he must face the spectre of the soup kitchen he says, "To hell with it, I'll do it myself." The "it" doesn't matter. It may be mixing cement, laying bricks, running the machine, driving the truck, stocking shelves, or shoveling sand. Whatever the job is, he knows he can do it as well as anyone else, so why not just buy his own equipment, or rent his own place, and go into business for himself?

DEVELOPMENT CYCLE
OF A BUSINESS

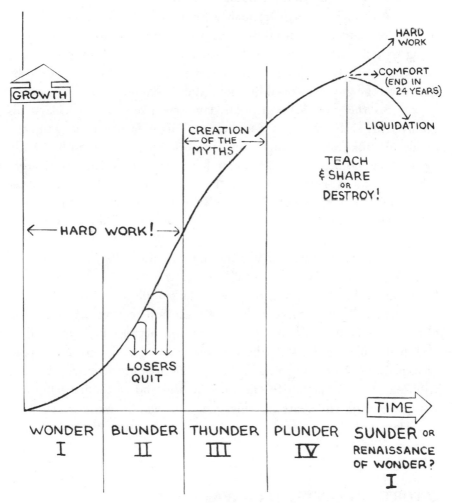

Figure 2.

Now, obviously, not every man became an owner manager in this way. For some the jungle of the public corporation became untenable so they traded that one for the greener jungle on the other side of the fence, their own business. Possibly, the owner manager inherited or married into a going business, and he had to find out how to work within the existing company structure. A small number of men started businesses because they had invented a better mousetrap or discovered how to square the circle, but no one would buy their idea. Frustrated, they did it themselves in order to show their detractors they weren't nuts.

Although his wife probably knows he's scared to death, the new entrepreneur tells himself he is a rugged individualist. No one is going to tell him how to lead his life. He wants freedom, power, the last word on how the job should be done. He knows how it should be done. It's the guy who fired him who didn't know.

So the founder works all day, seven days a week. For his family, this early period is a nightmare. His wife never sees him, the children think he's a stranger, and the dog bites him when he finally does come home. He is overextended, undermanaged, and scared. When he asks for help, he means, "Pick up a shovel," "Run the other machine," "Drive the other truck." "Do something useful." "Get dirty." His definition of helping is to get sweaty and do what he tells you.

The owner manager is pursuing a dream. What that dream is may not be exactly clear to him, but he has a sense of purpose about his business that allows him to survive the tumult and shouting of the early years. Often, however, his wife has not been told this dream, not because he wishes to keep it a secret but because he is generally a very inarticulate guy. When he can get by with it, he grunts instead of explaining. Not being a co-author of the dream, the entrepreneur's wife may have a very different view of him and of the hardship and struggle during the years in which the business grows more than he has. Her view is frequently shared in some measure by other members of the family.

OPPORTUNITY—MYTH OR DREAM?

Any sensitive wife knows that an entrepreneurial husband is scared. She knows he needs help, but he is not able to ask for it. He is not able to tell where it hurts to the people who really care and can do something about it. And his fear adds to her fear.

When he risks their last dollar on a business of his own, chances are she does not feel proud. She's terrified. Visions of unemployment, shame, and hunger dance through her head because she does not picture the freedom, power, and heroism of her husband's dream. Where he emerges from defeat with a sense of victory, she sees only the anger, the groping, the fright, the wheeling-dealing, the "robbing Peter to pay Paul" that this new venture requires. She does not understand the tradeoffs of time and companionship that her husband makes in order to nurture his business. For her it is a lonely, frightening period.

In many cases, of course, the husband needs her services as bookkeeper, clerk, scheduler, or answering service. In this capacity he can ask her for help because it fits his understanding of "help" as pitching in, getting tired, and getting dirty. But rarely does the founder of a business see "help" as the sharing of the dream and the easing of the mental pain. And so, though she may work alongside of him, the wife of a business owner usually feels alone and apart from his goals. In many cases, the marriage cannot survive this pressure.

The young, beginning business owner is often most exposed in his incompetence. Because he is struggling to stay alive at the same time that he is learning to run a business, his mistakes in judgment and interpersonal relationships tend to be overemphasized by those who observe him from outside the business. He is often regarded as foolish or a dreamer for having forfeited the security of a steady job to strike out on his own.

Because he must drive a tough bargain to keep his financial head above water, he is considered stubborn, ruthless, conniving or unethical. He will work at rock bottom rates to get started; shave his profit to stay employed; and his competitors consider him a cutthroat. Staying alive in the jungle without friends, he learns the tricks of living on his withholding, using the float to kite checks, and factoring receivables as shipments when they're still in process. Undercapitalized and overdrawn, the entrepreneur has learned to cut every corner to stay alive.

I call this the wonder period. The owner manager, when he stops to think about his problems, asks himself, "How did I get in this mess?" And his wife wonders why he doesn't quit and get a steady job! Thirty years later, in the nostalgic haze of two martinis, it is known as the good, old days. But while it is happening, it's hell.

He's one quarter man and three quarters worker. Many businesses are formed; few survive this period. The mortality rate is just awful.

Human gestation takes nine months. God, in His wisdom, designed it this way in order to prepare parents for the responsibilities of caring for their child. The gestation period of a family owned business is unknown, but it is finite. In some period of time this child will be conceived, born, nurtured, grow, and, too often, die. The basic problem of the privately held business is that it seems unable to perpetuate itself. The problem is congenital in that its roots lie in the very formulation of the business, the early methods of organization and capitalization.

EARLY ORGANIZATION AND CAPITALIZATION

The battles of the early years are fought in the foxholes of the basement, the garage, and the trunk of the car. While the founder operates a drill press in the garage, or keeps stock in the basement, and hopes the zoning commission doesn't shut him down, Mom learns to keep books on the kitchen table. She may never have heard of a balance sheet, and a P/L statement won't tell her how much cash there is to buy groceries, but somehow she manages to keep the bills paid and the family fed.

It doesn't take a fancy accounting system to do this, and more than a little work may be done on the barter system. Somehow they manage to keep building. The bank doesn't foreclose on the mortgage, and they begin to develop a pride in this business they have created. When the children are old enough to lick stamps and address envelopes, they are "employed." In order to survive, the "work" and the "profits" must be kept within the family. So the children and the relatives all come in at odd hours to help and to pick up a little extra money on the side. In some cases family members swap sweat and muscle for a needed job. Since the owner can't pay them much, he substitutes fancy titles for money, and plays upon their family loyalty to keep them involved. This early participation in the business provides them with tenure in later years when key management positions are up for grabs.

For some members of the family involvement takes a different route. Turned down by suspicious banks, afraid of the loan shark, and already overextended by creditors, the budding entrepreneur goes to the only money source he can trust; his family and friends. Family solidarity provides the dollars needed to keep the struggling ship afloat. These relatives become instant shareholders in an enterprise which might, with luck, pay off. Years later when the business becomes profitable, these same people exercise their uneducated clout over the control of the company.

While Mom struggles to keep the assets and liabilities straight in the black marble, paper-covered notebook from the five and dime, Dad discovers that he has suddenly enrolled in a special university run by the Internal Revenue Service where accounting is a mandatory subject. (I call it IRSU.) It has a high tuition rate, about 50% of the profits, but it does force the businessman to institute some kind of accounting system. Most of them would not have bothered to do so on their own. They catch on fast to techniques for passing the course and kidding the teacher. Unfortunately, most never learn much about the purpose and function of the subject matter. In this early period the name of the game is called stay alive, con the creditors, avoid taxes, and keep some of the cash to finance growth. The growth curve during the wonder stage is relatively slow. Maximum energy is involved in remaining in business.

THE BLUNDER PERIOD—STAGE TWO

But for those that survive, there is growth. And the owner manager enters middle age with a burgeoning business. He is still harassed, overworked and scattered in his efforts. He does everything wrong, but he does so much of it that it works out okay. He adds employees, relatives, creditors, and customers.

Some of his wife's fear begins to lessen in the blunder period. Although her husband is still the company's hardest working employee and he is almost a stranger to the rest of the family, there now is some money coming in. Immediate starvation seems unlikely, and the wolf at the door may even have become a small fox around the neck. She still finds her husband overworked and moody. Whatever is bothering him, he doesn't share it with her. His business crises are his own special area of pain whether they involve trouble with the union, scratching to outbid a competitor, fighting with a supplier for credit, or selling a customer a new line. When she tries to understand him, she is usually met with the stock answer, "Just keep my glass filled and my socks mended and we'll do OK."

His son grows up hearing Dad come home from the office blasting the unions, damning the government, shouting that his lousy competitors are cutthroats and that the help is stealing him blind. Then, in the next breath, he turns to his son and says, "Someday, my boy, all this is going to be yours." No wonder the poor kid decides to join the Peace Corps.

Unfortunately, during the blunder period, the owner's business personality also develops a tendency which will plague his later development. He becomes secretive. It's not just that he doesn't trust anyone else, although he really doesn't, it's that the founder sees his business as an extension of himself. I think of founders of businesses not as the fathers of their business but as the mothers. And, in mothering his business, the founder becomes overprotective of what he has created.

He may tell some people some things, and other people other things, and he may be willing to show his employees how their jobs should be done. But he never shares the total business picture with anyone. He knows the customers; he knows the suppliers; he knows the receipts and expenditures; he knows the payroll; and he thinks he knows his cost of "doing business."

Other people may know bits of this information because their jobs require it. But no one knows everything. He keeps things to himself. His 11th commandment is "Don't teach people nothin'." It's his business. He had the guts to build it from zero, and he can run it as he wants to. To his role of man and employee, he's added that of boss. The growth curve shoots upward during this period, often at a dizzying rate. The function of the founder begins to change.

He still works 18 hours a day, is rarely home, and has become very secretive about his business. Reasons for the secretiveness vary: fear that if the family realizes that he's on to a good thing, they'll try to cash in on his chips; fear that if his friends think he's a soft touch, they'll either pawn their no-good sons off on him or, worse still, hit him up for a loan; fear that if any of his employees knew how close to the brink he rode his business, they'd quit, or if they knew how much money he was making, they'd want a raise; fear that if the bank knew how close he is to the edge they'd call in his note; fear that if his advisors discover he's beginning to make money, they'd raise their prices; fear that if the union knows he's becoming successful, they'd want to negotiate a new contract. Whatever the reason, he doesn't trust anyone. Some people can know some things, and other people can know other things, but no one can know it all. And he makes sure that they don't.

Because his pride and his fear and his lack of trust in the wonder period made it impossible for him to ask for help from those who might have guided his efforts, the founder of a business learned mostly from trial and error. He was a protozoic pragmatist, reinventing the wheel each time he made a business decision. It didn't matter if his answer was right or wrong for the long run. What mattered was whether it worked then. He made so many decision so fast, and he made so many mistakes that enough were bound to turn out right in the end, so he prospered. Those things which did turn out right were called "management decisions." Suddenly he was the Boss.

It is during this period of rapid growth that the business owner finally begins to ask for help. He seeks advisors. He's making money, but he has accounting problems, so he looks for financial advice. He has difficulties with the union or with the IRS and he looks for legal advice. He may require cash to support expansion, so he looks for a banker. Unfortunately, he does not generally look for the best talent to advise him, just the most available and the most pliable.

I rarely meet men in these first two stages. They are too busy "working" to have time to spend with management philosophers.

Their idea of "help" is still to pick up the other shovel, drive the other truck, or take care of the other customer.

THE THUNDER PERIOD—STAGE THREE

By the time the business reaches its third stage of growth, the owner thinks he has it made. The curve becomes less dramatic, but the business is still growing, secure in the massive upward strides it has made during the blunder period. The owner has attained relative security, comfort, and a feeling that he's finally been able to show "them."

Here's where I usually start to meet the business owner at conventions. This is his period of instant business acumen. What he has built has grown. He's well-fed, well-dressed, sought after and respected by public and private organizations as client, patron and sponsor. The knockwurst and beans days are over. He thinks he's invented profits. His wife's diamond ring is safe on her hand; he's switched his line of credit from pawn shop to the bank. In fact, he may now even be on its board of directors. He can spend Christmas in the Caribbean and summers at the cottage in Canada. He's on the membership committee of the Club and his war stories are heard at the bar of the Sheraton-Waikiki. He's loud, obnoxious, and opinionated. This is his thunder period. He knows it all. He even understands you don't have to make a corporate profit to live well.

SUCCESS REARS ITS UGLY HEAD

It is during the thunder period that the sweat and strain of the business finally seem to pay off for Mom. Suddenly she has a husband with influence, affluence and power. There are expensive vacations, fashionable clothes, memberships in the best clubs, and a sense of position in the community. She still doesn't get more than a grunt from her husband in answer to her questions. He is still secretive about his operations, but there are material advantages to compensate for the years in which she trusted that it would all work out right.

The children find out that Dad has clout. He has influential friends. He has money. And he likes to spread it all around because it makes him feel good. Dad's earned the right, and they are his beneficiaries. The children go to the best schools, and the family drives company cars.

HAPPINESS IS CALLED "CONTROL"

During this phase, accounting practice becomes more than keeping books on the back of an envelope or borrowing on the cash value of the life insurance. Depending on whose advice he took at the time of incorporation, he did so to avoid personal liability, to gain preferential tax advantages, or to obtain additional capital without a personal guarantee. (i.e., so he could sell subordinated debentures to his brother-in-law and never have to pay him back.) The major reason for incorporation—to provide for the continuity of a going business beyond the lifetime of its founders—was not even considered at that point.

In this corporation, he is the major, if not the sole, stockholder. He has elected himself president. His family and friends may hold some shares. But they really aren't worth very much. Like a man told me, "Fifty-one percent of the stock in a family corporation is worth a helluva lot because with it you can elect yourself president. Forty-nine percent ain't worth nothin'."

Minority shares in a family business don't beef up a portfolio at all. A man can pass on to his son, his wife, his daughter, or his favorite charity, 100 shares of some blue chip stock and expect that the gift would be appreciated and valued per se. But what are 100 shares of Eureka Nut & Bolt worth to anyone but the President of Eureka Nut & Bolt if there are no "profits," and no market for the sale of the stock. No one can trade the shares of a family corporation; he can't buy them or sell them, except under some special circumstances. He probably doesn't even get much in the way of dividends from them because a family corporation does not seem to be in business to "make money." It seems to be in business to break even, higher and higher. Now that takes some pretty fancy accounting to do this, but it can be done, as any graduate of IRSU can tell you.

AN EXAMPLE MIGHT HELP EXPLAIN

A business acquaintance of mine in the midwest is a pilot. He took me out to his hanger one day and he showed me his plane. It was beautiful. Here was $125,000 worth of corporate aircraft. (I knew this had to be a corporate airplane, because I had a feeling for what this company generated in the way of profits, and he couldn't have afforded it on his net.) And this man owned a business which operated in a 12 mile radius.

After we were through flying around the countryside, we went to his office and we looked at the building, his equipment, and his inventory. I even asked to look at his financials. I really wanted to see where he had his airplane on the books, and I thought I knew where to look. I couldn't find it. Finally, I asked him, "Would you please tell me where you list this plane?"

And he said, "Right here."

And I read, "Transportation equipment, red truck TE."

I asked. "What is a red truck TE?"

And he said, "Shhh. That means twin engine."

As I said, a well run family business always seems to be able to break even higher and higher.

The practices of the privately owned business are directly tied to the tax laws of this country. Federal laws provide us the opportunity to take out all salary and expenses prior to any taxation on profit. As a result, the private business does not generate as much profit for distribution among shareholders as does a publicly owned business. Profit is much better translated into salaries and benefits distributed among members of the family. The family company can provide a good living for the owner without showing a need for a large profit.

CHARTS ARE ABORIGINAL ART

During the blunder-thunder periods, growth stretched beyond the boundaries of the family. Growth meant the addition of employees, and, consquently, the development of an organization in which outsiders supplied a large segment of the manpower. One of the ways of finding out how the owner manager feels about these non-family members is to ask him to draw an organization chart of his business. No document prepared by an owner manager ever gives a clearer indication of his management style than an organization chart. It is the ink-blot test for owners of family businesses. Most of these early charts resemble aboriginal art; they are plumber's nightmares. Dotted lines go everywhere. Everybody's job is connected to everybody else's job, and the Boss sees on his chart a beautiful interconnection between all these relationships.

But do you know what I see? I see something which looks like a big rake. Sitting on top of the handle is the head honcho, the Boss, and down at the bottom is "the help." (See Figure 3). He calls them the executive team. I call them corporate domestics.

If you look closely, you can usually find a line off to the left somewhere running to a box about halfway down with no name, going nowhere. That's where you find the son. Nobody's sure what his position means, but that's where you'll find him. And below that, a little farther out on another line, on the other side, and *lower*, is the son-in-law.

He may be a CPA with an MBA from Harvard and the son can be a congenital idiot, but the son-in-law is always lower on the chart. Dad insists on it. He never did like the gorilla who is sleeping with his baby.

SECRECY AND NON-REVIEW

But the most interesting part of these charts is finding the special box right beneath the President identifying the location of the 52-year old maiden lady with a moustache who keeps the books. That's not exactly true. Gertrude doesn't *keep* the books. She *hides* the books. Because if the "help" ever found out what the Boss doesn't know, they'd quit.

Her job is really to keep them dumber than he is and her major asset is called loyalty. (In actual fact, she's hanging on desperately to her job the only way she can because, if anyone else

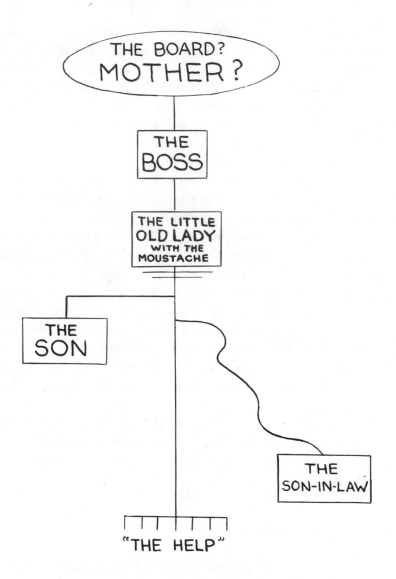

THE "**RAKE**"
FORM OF ORGANIZATION

Figure 3.

ever discovered what *she* doesn't know, she'd be through.) So some people learn some things, and other people learn other things. But nobody learns it all. Gertrude helps the boss see to that.

I call this secrecy. You may call it selective non-disclosure, but the result is the same. Nobody is really in a position to argue with the judgment of the owner-manager. This is called non-review. And it is this secrecy and this lack of review that are the hallmarks of the organizational structure of the family-owned business. This structure is firmly in place by the end of the second phase of growth in the family business.

Perhaps, this is an enlightened business owner. Somewhere he hears something about a thing called "management by objectives," "team approach," "cluster management." He decides which style really fits him best and he will tell you that he is delegating responsibility to various segments of his team.

That's nonsense! You cannot delegate responsibility without information and neither he nor Gertrude is going to risk full disclosure to "the team." So instead of looking like a rake, this guy has an organization chart that resembles a spider. He sits in the middle of the web and periodically goes out to confer with the plant foreman or the warehouse superintendent or the sales manager. But it is still "me" and "him", one-on-one. Nobody gets together to set objectives or compare data. So the result is the same. The corporate domestics, instead of being prongs on the rake, are bodies on the web. (See Figure 4) And buzzing around fruitlessly outside are the sons and the sons-in-law.

Nobody tells the boss he shouldn't behave that way. For employees to say so would be mutiny. Their jobs depend upon compliance with his basic management philosophy, "Shut up and do as I say." The longer they manage to live under this philosophy, the higher they climb in the business structure.

Loyalty and tenure provide the moves up the organization ladder. Competence has little or nothing to do with it. And besides, the employees are mostly trapped. They hold the best jobs they ever had. They never were managers anywhere else, and they have no skills which they can trade in the market place for the same kind of money they get in the family-owned firm. Consequently, the

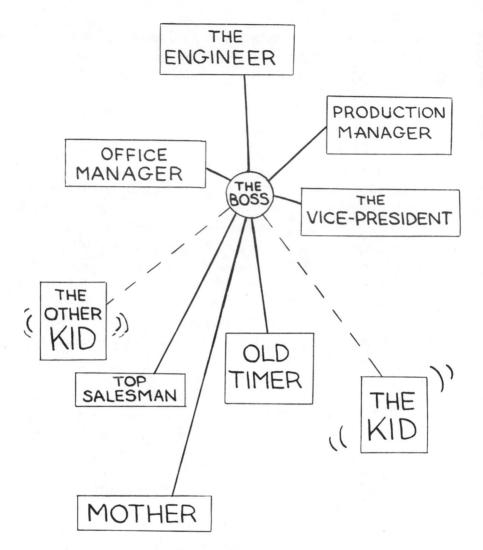

THE **"SPIDER"** FORM OF ORGANIZATION CHART

Figure 4.

business owner thinks he can hire whomever he needs to run the parts of his business without accounting to them for how the business functions as a whole.

By the time he reaches the thunder period, the business owner's money buys him position and status. Aware of his new social position, he uses it to make up for lost time. The living he has not been able to do as he was building the business, he tries to cram into extra-curricular achievements. In addition to his role as man, employee, and manager, he suddenly has become an investor. His fascination with the market provides a living for his broker.

As the business expands, the company is still too often dependent upon second-story legal talent, and accounting talent, and banking connections made when the operation was the size of a fruit stand. Advisors' fees have gone up to meet the owner's ability to pay, but the advisors don't know anything more, and they are never going to learn. Preying on, but never solving, a successful owner's fears will keep his advisors in business for the rest of their lives.

I try to avoid business owners at this stage. They are unpleasant. They want you to think they have the world by the tail. They don't realize that they are getting into trouble and they tell you nobody can help them. To cover up the fact that they don't really understand how to function as president and chief executive officer, business owners invent and believe five myths about their business.

MYTH ONE—"MY BUSINESS IS DIFFERENT"

When any outsider discusses management practices with a business owner, he is told that *"my business is different."* This is the stock answer to any question about why he doesn't do this, or why he does that, or what is the net long term effect upon his business of some specific business practice? As a statement, it is true. His business *is* different, but not for the reasons he advances. His business is different because it is so uniquely designed, so custom fitted to the individual expertise of the founder that no one else can run it.

What good is genius if it is not teachable or transferable? Where horse and rider are so uniquely suited to each other, how does one transfer riders if no one else can ride them? This is what makes it different. And yet the successful business owner is so perverse and so vain that when no one can ride the horse he has trained, he blames everyone except the trainer. In the end, the only solution is often to shoot the horse.

When the company is doing well, it is because of the founder's ability; when it is doing badly, it is because of circumstances, the environment, the government, and the unions. The owner president lives in his own private world. He is a lonely man. He has no one with whom he can be honest about his problems. He can't tell his employees, his wife or his partners. He is a successful man, but he is pedestrian, parochial, and managerially illiterate. He is a lonesome, able, powerful guy. His problems are unique. His business is different. He made it that way. Strangely enough, the business of all owner managers is "different" in exactly the same way.

MYTH TWO—"WHEN YOU'VE HAD MY EXPERIENCE, YOU'LL UNDERSTAND"

The second myth which the business owner believes is that he doesn't need to change his business practices now because his many years of experience have qualified him to run his company exactly as he want to have it run. This point of view is especially hard on his wife, his heirs, and the members of his management staff. While he has been building the business, the world has changed. Yet, he does things the way he has always done them, the only way he knows how. Suggestions for changes in management, products, or markets are met with the growl, "It's my business. We'll do it my way." And he successfully seals off criticism. Who in the organization has been at it as long as he has, or dares to contradict his power.

Superimposed upon the growth curve of business, however, is another curve, a curve of competence which is measured both in time and complexity. The company is nearing the top of its growth curve with a tremendous increase in scale. At the same time, the world has not stood still. There has been an increase in complexity. (See Figure

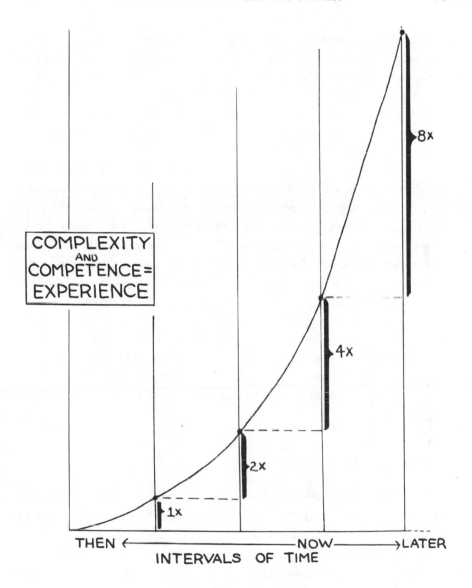

COMPLEXITY
AND
COMPETENCE=
EXPERIENCE

8x

4x

2x

1x

THEN ← ——————————— NOW ——→ LATER

INTERVALS OF TIME

EXPERIENCE=
? YEARS

Figure 5.

5) It is an exponential curve that gets increasingly complex. With the passage of time, a man's competence is measured by his ability to withstand and live with complexity. To be blunt, this means that past "experience" becomes less and less relevant or valuable. The simplicity of experience required to maintain competence at the bottom of the curve is not of much value in the complexities of larger scale at the top of the curve.

So when an owner-president hangs on for 25, 30, or 40 years, his time span in a rapidly changing technology is, for the most part, useless. His vaunted experience isn't worth much. It's not 30 years experience; it may just be 10 years experience, three times. Or 15 years experience, twice. Or, in some terrible cases, maybe two years experience, 15 times. But it sure isn't thirty years experience, and it is hard to tell that to a man who has been successful most of his life. Thirty years experience in the presidency of the Eureka Supply Company is not particularly valuable or relevant in a rapidly changing world. But I don't try to tell him this during his myth-building, thunder stage. He won't listen in the first place. And, in the second place, he's so busy inventing profit and enjoying success, that it would be a damn shame to tell him how soon it may all go bust.

MYTH THREE—"IT'S MY MONEY"

The next myth which develops during the thunder period is "It's my money, and it's my business how I spend it." Unfortunately, that just isn't true. For one, Uncle Sam has some interest in how he spends his money; where he keeps it; and how he tries to hide it. Unless he has first-class financial advisors, he's going to fail miserably at making the money work for him, his company, and his old age.

And other people have an interest in what he does with his money. His employees and his managers need to feel that the money from the business is being used to strengthen the business. His family needs to know that the family fortune is in good hands and protected as much as possible from error, his or any other.

Family members are not much inclined to look favorably upon a use of "their money" which does not include "their future." Though it may have been a pittance at the time, some of the capital that started the business may have come from Aunt Helen or Uncle Morton and their outstretched hands today are not satisfied merely with a pittance in return! They feel their money has bought them a sense of "control" over company decisions and a "right" to a return on their investment.

MYTH FOUR—"BUSINESS IS LOUSY"

When pressed to disavow the myths he has so busily constructed, the business owner will try to con you into believing a fourth myth, "it's not so great to own your own business. I should never have done it." He'll tell you, "Our business is tough. Our competitors are vicious. Foreigners have invented a process that will put us out of business. Our suppliers have us over a barrel. The union is moving in. We only made one and one half percent on sales last year. I should have kept my money in the bank." And where will he be when he confides all this? At the bar at the Acapulco Hilton. The truth is that wherever it comes from and wherever it ends up, somehow money is generated and enjoyed and used. Given the chance and the challenge, he'd do it all over again.

MYTH FIVE—"IT'S MY BUSINESS . . . I'LL DO WHAT I WANT WITH IT"

If no one will fall for myth number four, he has another in his hip pocket ready to scare family and employees alike. "This is my business," he'll say. "I built it myself and if I want to, I can sell it out or close it up." That usually makes the hair of even the most mutinous doubter stand on end. It shuts him up for good. What value is his inheritance, or his job, if the old goat closes up shop, takes his marbles, and moves off into a permanent sunset in the Caribbean or California?

But, if he does close it up, what is he going to do with himself? If he slowly liquidates it, what makes him think that it can remain profitable exactly long enough so he can go to his eternal reward just *before* the whole thing collapses on him? Who does he really think is going to bail him out at a premium price?

This problem is three-fold. How much is a family business worth to anyone outside the family? Who wants to buy a corporation that exists as much in the head of its owner as on the books in the accountant's office? What is there to sell, really, in most family organizations which have been built to accommodate the peculiarities of one man? Not a whole lot, unless there has been some real move towards continuity of the business. Some inventory. The receivables. A store. A warehouse. Some trucks. Equipment. All worth about 15¢ on the dollar if placed on the auction block. That won't provide a very glorious retirement for a man accustomed, now, to the best. So, although he may scare the hell out of the young hot bloods in his organization with statements like this, he really is not going to act on that myth, either.

SUNDER OR PLUNDER—OR NEW WONDER—THE FOURTH STAGE

By the time he is 50, 55 or 60, depending largely upon the age at which he got involved in his business, the founder has usually become disenchanted with this flamboyant thundering stage. If this was his most unpleasant period, the last stage is, perhaps, both the saddest and the most dangerous time of all. The change in his personality has not changed his belief in his immortality. It is in this stage, therefore, that he can destroy on the way down the business which he built on the way up. Depending upon how he responds to it, this stage is one either of plunder, sunder, or a rebirth of wonder. By this time, the growth curve generally begins to level off.

As a man reaches 60, the wear and tear begin to show. Even though he may think he is going to live forever, Mom and the children recognize that he is getting old. He begins to get stodgy, sleeps late on Sunday; plays golf at a slower pace; takes a shine to health foods, fad diets, and a new wardrobe to keep his youth. He becomes more conservative not only in his politics but in his business. He just wants to keep things on an even keel—keep the business going as usual—but he doesn't want to try anything new. He's lost his appetite for risk. To his son, the old man is an impediment, a road block to progress who won't really let him have any responsibility in the business. The boy wants to climb but Dad's stock answer to any suggestion of growth is, "When you've had the years of experience that I've had, then you can change things."

Mom is caught in the middle, between the man she's watched drive himself mercilessly to "success" and the son who wants to make his mark in the world. Dad probably couldn't beat his heir in a fair fight anymore, so he achieves his domination through a tight hand on the purse strings and through a control of information about the business. It's a little like the old high school athlete who teaches his son his favorite sport and each year takes pride in what his boy can do—"taught him everything he knows." Then when the day comes that his son beats him at his own sport, what does dad say then? "I'm off my game today, son." It's no wonder that in this period those who love him, the family for whom he has built this kingdom, react in a mixture of respect, fear, envy, and frustration for he is, after all, the keeper of the keys.

For all of them, Mom, Dad, and the kids, this is a difficult time. Dad doesn't want to quit; Mom is afraid that his constant work will kill him before his time; and the kids are afraid that if he doesn't quit, only his death will give them a chance. Many businesses die along with their owners because this conflict is not resolved in the owner's lifetime. He takes the keys to the kingdom with him into his box in the ground.

Age suddenly has become a partner in the family business. Without investing a penny, Age can become the controlling shareholder and the manner in which the founder deals with himself determines the course of the business. No one wants to quit. Men want to believe that they will die with their boots on, get shot in the saddle, or succumb gloriously in battle. No gutsy, sweaty, fighting, individualistic, rough and tumble, built-it-myself businessman believes he will die in bed of old age. It isn't heroic. It isn't patriotic. It may even be unAmerican. Frontiers weren't defended that way.

The sad fact is that all of us must at some point face our own obsolescence. All pilots must land. They do a better job if they do it before, not after, they run out of gas. The business owner finds himself caught between his fear of retirement and his desire for comfort, for enjoyment, for reaping the rewards of his labor. He does not voluntarily consider retirement. He equates it with euthanasia. Therefore he lives out his declining years fearful of aging, fearful of change, and fearful for the stability of his business. He is unclear about his role in the business. He is constantly buffeted between the four parts of his world. He is confused about his objectives and fearful that his dream will not live after him. He is cautious about continuing to build his business. His sense of risk is gone. If his managers or his heirs come to outline new plans, to propose opening new territories, to recommend new products or services, to suggest new risks and rewards, he has a stock answer; "Not with my money, you don't."

In his desire to live out his last years in splendor, he dreams of converting his assets into cash. He really has three choices: (1) At his death, his executors can liquidate what little remains from his neglect; or (2) If he is no longer able to work at his own pace, if keeping up with change causes more pain than pleasure, if the demands of the business override his leisure and enjoyment, then he will try to get his money out of the business and enjoy what years remain. He will try to sell out, merge, close-up, or "go public." In any event, he will try to sunder his relationship with his business.

But there is a third alternative. That is the possibility of investing his successors with his own sense of wonder in the joy of risking and building the business so that they can provide the leadership the business needs to continue to grow, without repeating all the mistakes and hardships of a first generation. This is what I term the rebirth of wonder . . . the real solution to the continuity of the owner managed business.

Chapter Four

The Who's Who of Power

THE WHO'S WHO OF POWER

A description of the family owned business would not be complete without an inside look at the "family." The business owner did not construct his company in a vacuum. He built it within the very real and influential environment of a family. The future of the business is as haunted by the existence of the family as the past of the business depended upon it. No other single characteristic of a privately owned business distinguishes it so completely from the publicly held company as the influence of the family upon the nature, scope, and future of the business. Too few professional managers understand the position which the family plays in the policymaking functions of the business. Professional men who seek to advise presidents of family companies are too often ignorant of the pressure of family undercurrents which can influence the decisions within the company.

In its interrelatedness of family functions and company organization, the family business is the X-rated movie of the economic world. No one is allowed in unless accompanied by a

47

parent. Nowhere on the organizational charts of public corporations are there job descriptions entitled "son," "son-in-law," "relative," and/or "old friend." Since these roles are almost unique to the family business, they function as a position as well as relationships. To understand and appreciate the complexity of a privately owned corporation, therefore, it is necessary to have a feel for these characters and the parts they play in the operation of the company. The importance of each role varies in individual businesses, but few companies exist without such a cast. The variations on personality are infinite. I will cite just a few of them. The business owner should feel free to adjust or redesign the characteristics among the parts to conform to his own family.

1. *Old Dad*: He is the hairy-chested mesomorph who founded the business and built it from a one truck, one shovel, one machine, one location operation to what it is today. He is the self-appointed leader of a dynasty. Endowed with a hide that will ward off crocodiles, he is secretive, confused, harassed, non-reviewed, insular, pedestrian, parochial, powerful, tired, scared, lonely, and running out of time. Assuming his position on the basis of power and not merit, he has a desire to perpetuate a dream which he has founded and looks to his children as heirs and successors. The son who will succeed him is "the kid" at home and "the help" at work. Dad tells him nothing and rarely shares the responsibility for running the business with him, and then wonders why the boy is never quite ready to take over. Highly skilled in his particular field, Dad is a poor manager and mostly inarticulate. His job will cease only when he retires, which is unlikely, or when he dies—which he doubts.

I once had an 89 year old man attend a seminar of mine. When it was over, he told me how much he'd enjoyed himself. "I really want you to get hold of my boy," he said. "He's not catching on to the business at all."

"Fine," I answered. "How old is the lad?"

"Fifty-seven," he answered.

Another old fellow who had brought his 51 year old son with him celebrated his 81st birthday on the first day of one of our seminars. After informing us of this fact at lunch that day, he told me that it was his practice to have a nap from 1 to 3 every day and asked would I mind if he napped after lunch. "Of course not," I said with understanding. I'll never forget his parting words as he left the seminar on his way back to his room, "Don't anybody say anything important until I get back!"

2. *Momma*: Often Dad's first employee and bookkeeper, she also functions as major recruiting agent for the second generation of the business. When Dad incorporated, she became the mainstay of the board of directors and used her power and influence to push the son into a position of sheltered status within the company. As the business becomes successful, she may view it as the family cow to be milked for the pleasure of the family because either 1) she has never been invited to share the dream which is the destiny of the business, or 2) she feels she deserves some cream after all her hard work. At Dad's death she becomes the matriarch of a dynasty in a world she barely understands. To cover her ignorance she permits the business to be run by self-appointed Richelieus and Rasputins—advisors and managers-who direct the company through the frontal power of Momma. Political intrigue within the company then centers around the pressures of the relatives and successors to remove Momma and Rasputin from their position of power before the business withers and to install competent successors in management. In addition to the real Momma, other elderly ladies may get involved, old aunts, first wives, and Grandma, all usually widows (or divorced) and, more often than not, represented by trust officers and attorneys on contingency. These ladies like to come in to meetings, however, and feel "left out" if their opinions are not asked on all matters in which they have an interest; raises, promotions and the assignment of both status and work.

3. *Relatives*: These include both sides of the family, dad's brother's cousins, mom's sister's boy and assorted members of the "other family," usually leftover from earlier "partnerships"—inlaws and outlaws—sometimes friendly to each other but usually jealous as hell of the "benefits" enjoyed by the members of "the other family." They are often an early source of financial backing and usually the first employees after Dad and Mom. If still working for the company, they have probably outgrown their usefulness, but, because they are family, they cannot be fired without straining the

relationships outside the working world. Even if they are not on the payroll, they still enjoy milk from the family cow. Their sense of "entitlement" is based on early participation in the form of capital, manpower, or familial relationship. They expect a good return on their "investment" in the form of cash, fringe benefits, or employment.

4. *Sons*: No one is sure what the job of "son" is, but in the family-owned business it is as real as any other. The son wakes up every morning conscious that his father owns the business and that someday he may inherit it. He is faced from early childhood with the decision, "Will I accept the job?" and the fear, "Will it ever be given to me?" The pressure of the choices can cause two extreme behaviors: 1) He can become overly involved in concepts of business administration in order to be "prepared" for his responsibility; 2) he can become guilty about the fact that Dad, the Boss, provides a good life of which he never feels worthy, causing him to drop out and become a socialist, a revolutionary, a dilettante or a greedy, intellectual bum. He becomes a non-economic being who assumes that his position in the family will assure him of an income even though he does not accept the responsibility. Whatever his choice, he will be conscious his whole life of being a "son." Consequently, sons tend to be over-sold and under-developed. No one has any sympathy for "sons," and few people understand their problem. After all, the kid was born with a silver spoon and inherited a gold mine. If he succeeds, it was because Dad built a good thing, and all the son had to do was keep it running. If he fails, it's because he wasted his birthright in riotous living, was stupid, or a playboy.

Sons need to be tested. They need an opportunity to succeed on their own, before they assume control of the family business. Unfortunately, they rarely get this chance, so they suffer through life with a sense of emasculation, a sense of inadequacy, a sense of lack of merit, which they only admit out loud when they have had too much sauce. Sons without hangups are all too rare.

5. *Daughters*: As long as there is a son as successor, nobody really expects a daughter to do anything except inherit a portion of the stock. Should the business owner have no male progeny, however, or should the son drop out, the daughter could through

marriage be the chief recruiter of a successor to the business. A daughter may suffer, however, if she marries a competent man who enters a business in which her brother succeeds to the presidency. She will always be in a stepped-down position in relation to her brother and his wife, because her husband's title will always be lesser than her brother's. Dad usually sees to that.

Of course in this new era of equal rights and womens lib—maybe competent daughters can more easily become presidents of family businesses in their own right.

6. *Sons-in-law*: They usually have grown up as regular kids without an executive playpen or sandbox in which to play. Their fathers usually did not have the privilege of awarding them sheltered positions free from rebuff or criticism. They probably learned enough from their education to prove their competence in a job they acquired on the basis of merit, so they have had some assessment of their own ability. They expect and accept outside review. It is not until they happen to marry a nice girl that they suddenly discover they have married into a business. If there is no son, a son-in-law may become president (otherwise he is always executive vice-president) but he can rarely become a shareholder because he is not family. He just sleeps with a major potential shareholder and Dad worries if someday the gorilla may divorce his baby. Sons-in-law are either considered very good at what they do or very bad. They are never average. The son-in-law is in the unique position of great talent or minimal talent taking tremendous advantage of a situation by the accident of marriage. On any organization chart of a family business in which there is a son and a son-in-law, the son-in-law is never treated as an equal regardless of his ability. Sons of Sons-in-law are in an even worse position. They belong to the "other family." They are treated even less equally than sons-in-law. Their jobs (if they inherit jobs at all) are usually handed out on the basis of need or clout, not ability.

7. *Wives of Sons*: They hold a competitive position based upon their husband's rank within the company. Since succession is awarded on the rule of primogeniture, wives generally reflect the status their husbands have achieved not by relative merit but by order of birth. The wife of an older brother maintains the uppermost

status because her husband is usually the president. Other wives obtain status in direct relation to their husbands' familial positions, although they constantly compete for advantages which they assume the wives above them already have. In most cases, the competition is dirty and ill-fated. The outcome was decided at birth.

It is the unusual family in which the daughters-in-law (married to the sons of the founder) don't feel superior to the daughter. After all, *her* husband is the president. If you don't believe me, ask the "girls" in the family business to draw an organization chart.

As seen by the daughter-in-law:

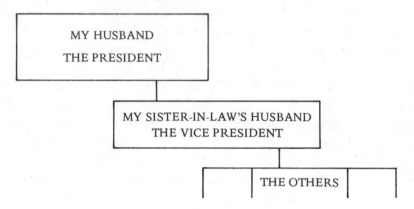

As seen by the daughter:

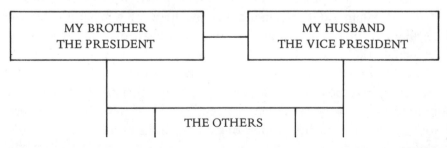

This can get pretty complicated in large families and the complexity is compounded in the transfer of stock and board memberships.

8. *Sibling Rivalries*: These take on the aspect of characters because of the intensity with which they affect the functioning of the business. Since the family businesses are like monarchies, the

oldest brother naturally becomes president, and succeeding brothers or husbands of sisters assume roles based on order of birth which itself established service time in the company. Comparative ability is too often a second consideration. The oldest son may be a perpetual drunk and the youngest a mathematical wizard. This does not alter their positions in the company. Similar inequities occur when the bright sister of two stupid, lazy brothers marries a competent, intelligent, hard-working man. Chances of his becoming president over the two brothers are 1000 to 1 against him. All kinds of sibling rivalries develop—between older brother and younger brother; between hard-working brother and lazy brother; between bright brother and stupid brother; between athletic, outgoing brother and shy, introverted brother. All are compounded and abetted by the wives of the gladiators. When both enter the family business where the toys are to be shared equally, they may end up working out their childhood aggressions with the company rattles. There are no schools of business administration for dealing with these kinds of strains, no books to read, and the psychiatrists don't understand business. Harmony usually lasts only as long as old Dad is alive and in charge and can maintain his position as family elder. His children are loathe to accept lower assignments within a hierarchy of contemporaries with "equal rights." The company may come apart in the process. The only way to guarantee a success in this area is to be the competent only son of an only son.

9. *Greedy Kids*: The family line-up doesn't always have to picture "the old man" as obsolete, incompetent, and hanging on forever, while all the young wear halos and are invariably cast as eager, hard-working, respectful, dedicated and the only hope for the future. It is not necessarily so. Unfortunately some heirs and heirs-in-law are overly impressed by their academic, marital or calling-card credentials. They can't wait for "the old man" to die off, and, if he doesn't do it soon enough, some attempt to make non-negotiable demands for "control" out of all proportion to their contribution. (Sometimes they even go so far as to use the grandchildren as hostages for compliance.) Greedy sons and daughters are bad enough (and their parents have to accept a share of the blame) but my heart goes out to the entrepreneur whose child

marries a greedy mate. All hopes or plans for a secure and satisfactory future are compromised and the inevitable family fights usually destroy both the business and the family. It's usually far better to get rid of them and regroup than to try to buy "love" with blackmail.

10. *Family Managers*: "The Help:" Mostly characterized by long service, they lack managerial experience anywhere else. Thoroughly convinced by the boss that their business is unique, they reinvent the management wheel. When young sons or sons-in-law come into business, managers tend to see them as threats to their positions. Rarely understanding that the heir's success is their greatest job security, they make bad jokes about him. Like the regent who always wanted to be king, they (and the little old lady with the moustache) would poison the little prince if they could. Sometimes put on "the board," they rarely know how to act. (Neither they nor the boss have ever seen any other board in action). Sometimes they become investors. (Just a few shares makes them think they are "partners"). They see their holdings as job security. Suspicious of any changes in the status quo, they generally resent any outsiders to "their business" or people who question their suggestions. This is the best job and the most money that they ever had. They are essentially immobile, and they fear that any change will leave them worse off than they are now. They consider the company as a club for senior members only.

11. *Advisors*: Enter a mixed bag of Rasputins—the lawyers, accountants, bankers, insurance agents, consultants, and other hangers-on who have been with Dad since the good old days. Their services came cheap in the period when he had few available dollars, and their limited talent was not overstretched. Too many never developed substantially beyond that early period, but they are kept on because of their "devotion" and "loyalty." Their influence is immense, and in the final stages of the founder's life it may be crucial. They succeed to a unique power should Dad kick off before a successor is trained and enthroned, especially if Momma, who is unprepared to do so, assumes control of the business. They become trustees of the family cow when Momma needs "help." They stand too often to gain most by "unpreparedness" in assuring corporate continuity. Liquidations can be profitable to them.

12. *Directors*: In any true sense they are mostly non-existent in the average family business. These positions are usually fictional, filled by relatives, friends, and other co-conspirators and self-servers. Their ability to function as a real power of review is limited 1) by their relationship to the family, 2) by their lack of information, and 3) by their probable incompetence in the first place.

Because of the intermesh between family roles and organizational roles, the real maneuvering of a family business takes place not so much in the 8-10 hours of the working day as in the 14-16 hours "at home." Board meetings become sessions in the boudoirs of the corporation legitimized only by the sham of the annual meeting in the lawyer's office.

Some family businesses think they have a real board if they add their various managers to it. This isn't a board, it's a management committee. Such a committee can be a very good idea of and by itself, but it is not to be dignified by the term "directors." Too often such board memberships are a "reward" for loyal service by grateful employees. Disagreement or challenge to concepts held by the old man results frequently in their becoming disloyal, ungrateful, ex-employees.

The quality of director relationships off the job affects the president's ability to function on the job and influences greatly the quality of decisions which are made about the business and its future. Failure by professional managers to understand this dimension of a privately-held business results in many of the other tensions between public corporations and their suppliers and distributors. Where a publicly owned corporation thinks it retains a man on the basis of his evaluated ability and merit, the privately owned corporation is loyal to relatives and long term employees regardless of their competence. The publicly owned company must adjust to these factors in dealing with the family business, if the survival of that business is crucial to the public company's success.

13. *Investors*: These are the real "insiders" in any family business. Before any substantive action is recommended by anyone outside this group, he had better understand who owns what, where people fit in the family tree, who they are, how they got "in," who wants what, and who gets what.

In addition to "the family" which collectively controls the majority of shares, one may find a variety of minority interests exercising clout in direct proportion to their holdings: "partners" from the first generation and their heirs, retired employees (with or without sell-back requirements), advisors who bought and took shares as their "interest" in the company, in the old days, (Now try to change advisors!); and sometimes, old "friends" who were "let in" on a good thing at some point. They have never seen any dividends but they like being "owners."

Needless to say, each of these investors sees "his company" as something different. And so do all the others: Dad, Momma, the kids, the relatives, the help, and the second guessers. You can't watch the game without a program.

Those outside of the family owned business observe the pressures and tensions of this interplay between family and business like the intrigue in a B movie, without any compassion and even less understanding because it's so badly written, and the critics have assured them it's bad. Many of these outsiders, advisors, customers, suppliers, employees and friends never see the two parts of the business owner's life as a complete whole. They see him either as a man with a business or a man with a family. They are not privy to the delicate balance between these two lines. They never bothered to understand his past. And often, therefore, they see only those negative or bizarre qualities which become exaggerated out of proportion, when they are not seen as part of the total texture of a man's life.

As a teacher and counsellor I have met thousands of owner managers in all kinds of business fields. I have known their families, their advisors, their friends and their enemies. I know the pictures that I draw of their perceptions are not exaggerated. I would like to think I have come to know these men and their families better than most, and a little more objectively. By the time I meet them, they are usually in their 50's, and much of the rough period is behind them. Their past is now their strength. Obviously there are notable exceptions to the rule. All of us can recount war stories about the unscrupulous businessman, if we are asked to. In general, however, when I look at the business founder and his business, this is what I see.

A SUCCESSFUL MAN

I see a man who has made it largely as the result of his own efforts, his own errors as well as his own successes. He is hard-working, a fighter, and basically a very ethical and honest man. I see a man who is surprised by his own success and unsure just what to do about it. He has built this great business and now he doesn't know what to do with it. He is afraid it will all disappear, and he has come to love it and identify it as a part of himself. He wants it to survive him, to be his immortal dream.

I see a man who is also fearful of the effort and the work that is required just to hang on. But, because he fears that the business will die if he does not manage it, he will not give it up. He compensates for being scared and tired by fooling himself into believing he is divine. And others support this view of him through their dependence or their greed.

I see a man who is managerially untutored. He has been so busy building the business that he's never had time to find out what it means to be a manager. Not only is his managerial experience limited, so is his world experience. This is a man who is parochial and immobile. Although of late he travels the world as a tourist, he has lived and worked in the same place his whole life. He has a basic mistrust of the mobile professional manager who changes jobs and towns with seemingly little or no effort. He is a pillar of his community because he must live there. His wife must live there and his kids grow up there. If his money and energy can make it a good place to live, then he's willing to shell out to insure that the town stays the way he likes it.

Finally, I see a man who is basically inarticulate. He has never had to explain anything to anyone. He has always done it his way. Right or wrong, he did it the way he wanted to, and anyone who didn't like the way he flew his plane could get out at any time. So not only does he not explain things, he does not know what he should explain or how to do it. When stuck for an answer, he grunts—or says, "Ya know what I mean?" And you're supposed to say, "yes" so he doesn't think you're stupid.

By the time I finally meet this owner manager, he is becoming aware of the crucial nature of the problem of succession in the business. It is best for both of us if I meet him early in the final sunder-plunder-wonder period. I don't practice on hopeless cases. Unless the owner is willing to accept change and to make some plans for continuity well before the end of this period, his disease is terminal.

In the businesses which I have known during this period of their life cycle, I have found that, for the most part, the problems are duplicated over and over again. The business structure is a neolithic implement polished by 24 years of cultivated ignorance. A million dollar business operates by a hip-pocket, back-of-the-envelope organization chart. It lacks first rate advisors; it lacks a competent outside board of directors; it lacks a known and qualified successor; it lacks an informative accounting system; it lacks managers with commitment and challenge. It's become a one-owner creature—like a horse that won't accept any other riders. The founder won't get thrown off the horse. No one will steal the horse. It's just that the horse will probably die under him. Or that the rider will get too fat to ride him.

THE 30 YEAR DYNASTY

But no two-fisted, blockbuster of a business owner wants to admit that the day will come when he won't/can't run the business. When does the old goat plan to step down? Never. I have yet to meet a business owner who has authorized a legally binding document which says that on any given date, under any given conditions, he is going to retire without being an approving party to the event when it happens. Not one of them, I'm sure, has an irrevocable retirement plan. I don't mean deferred income, the board chairmanship, a consulting job with the company. I mean retirement—stepping down—out. But he doesn't usually talk about retirement because he sees it as a form of castration. That's unfortunate. I think that the more competent a man is in his chosen profession, the more important it is that he decide, at the height of his powers, on a date on which he will confer his authority to another . . . his chosen heir.

By an heir I mean either the natural son or daughter who wishes to run the business, or else those adopted heirs to whom the business could fall in the case of no available biological heir. These could be the key managers who wish to continue the dream of the founder. Whatever the actual relationship of the heir to the owner, his role in the continuity of the business must be clear both to him and to the owner, and, during this phase of the business, his participation in preparing for the presidency is vital.

In my speeches, I often tell my audience that none of them has an irrevocable retirement plan. And at the end of the session or at the coffee break, it never fails that some old fellow comes up to me and says, "You know, Doctor, I didn't want to interrupt because I knew what you were getting at. But I do have a plan for retirement. I'm on it right now. I'm sort of semi-retired. I get to the office a little later, now. I read the mail, dictate some letters, go over some bills, take a couple of hours for lunch at the club, and play golf with my doctor on Wednesdays. In the afternoon I look around the plant a little bit, sign my mail and the checks, and leave early. The boys are really getting the hang of it and doing a wonderful job. And Mom and I go down to Florida or the islands in the winter for a couple of months. I hardly ever call them to check. I'm semi-retired. It's wonderful."

That's what he tells me. But do you know what I hear? I hear that as age has loosened his plate and it doesn't fit as well as it used to, and he can't hear as well as he once did, and his glasses are slipping down on his nose, and he can't wear all the suits in his closet, and he can't eat all the food in his icebox and he can't drink all the booze in his cellar, and both his golf game and his sex life are deteriorating, the only thing he has left in life he can count on is to go to the office, bang on the table, intimidate the help, alienate the customers, and foul up the business part time. This is what he calls "semi-retirement." You should hear what his employees and successors call it!

THE RACE BETWEEN OBSOLESCENCE AND RETIREMENT

A lifetime isn't something infinite, stretching from childhood to senility. It's more like 600 months, 50 years of conscious, working lifetime. Although he would like to believe he is divine, the owner manager cannot live out the ultimate myth, his own immortality. He is going to die. But the great tragedy is that many business owners manage their businesses in the levelling off period as though they thought they were going to live forever. They use the business and the funds it can generate to secure the comfort and enjoyment that they have missed during the other periods of growth.

They don't want to continue to climb. They just want the plane to level off and cruise at a pleasant speed so that they can enjoy the countryside as they fly over it. At this stage, what the owner manager would really like to do is to sort of keep up with the trend in the GNP—up 5-6% per annum. If he had his way, he'd hold the plane steady, or maybe let it nose up just a little bit and slow it down. He'd really like to collect his receivables faster than he generates them. He'd like to have his capital reinvestment remain lower than his depreciation, and have his inventory consumed faster than he can replenish it. He wants to be liquid—to have the comfort of cash in the bank so that he can have lunch with his bankers, pick up the tab, and vote Republican with a clear conscience.

It would be a nice, pleasant, comfortable way to live, except he has to be very careful how fast he converts his assets into cash. If he does it too quickly, it's called liquidation. What the owner manager really wants by this time is pure comfort, not because he is lazy, or indifferent, or greedy, but because he is tired; he is lonely; and he is afraid.

THE RECURRING NIGHTMARE

Today's business owner founded his company shortly after The War. His beliefs and his values were formed by his action in that war, whether his contribution was on the beach of Iwo Jima or walking a dog on the beach at Coney Island. And if he participated in The War, he has to remember the trauma of The Depression. So this man knows the value of hard work, shoring up his defenses . . . and guarding his money. And a gnawing fear that never quite diminishes no matter how affluent he becomes is that somehow, someday, he will wake up and it will all be gone. It's the recurring nightmare, even when he is wide awake.

His successor, on the other hand, does not remember The War. Chances are he may not even have been alive at that time. His memories of the early struggle to create the business are only the remembrance of an absentee father, a steady diet of spaghetti, and

Saturday mornings spent stacking shelves or shovelling sand. Much of the real toil is just an obscure shadow from the past floating over today's affluence, so when Dad tells him, "Boy, things were really tough," he shrugs and answers "Oh, sure." But that answer is not comforting to Dad. It never convinces him that his son really appreciates the struggle and the anger and the fear that built this business in which Dad takes such pride. Just as he fears that his daughter will run off and marry a barefoot, long-haired, guitar player, he's afraid his own son will destroy this other child, the product of his dream.

WHY RISK WHAT YOU HAVE FOR WHAT YOU DON'T WANT?

What frequently happens is that Dad's memory of the long hours and the hard work of the first three phases of the business hits the time and space and affluence conflict of the fourth period. In this confrontation, he is caught in the bind of knowing that something must be done about the business, but he is too tired to start building again. He's afraid to risk his hard-earned cash on an untried scrub team quarterback. So, instead of coaching his successor to take over the duties full time, he cops out and tries to avoid making a binding decision about the future of his business. Although he may place the blame for indecision on the lack of a work ethic in the current generation . . . rather than recognizing his own unwillingness to step down . . . his business is facing disaster.

Just as Dad sees the world through one concept of history, his son views it from a totally different perspective. His understanding of the world was focused closer to the top of the complexity curve while Dad's was formed in a less complicated jungle, near the bottom of the curve. New pressures on business from government, new legislation related to employment and taxation, the effects of civil rights, womens' lib, consumerism, and the ecology movements, are a familiar environment for the son. He has grown up during the formative period of these pressures. He may even have exercised his youthful exuberance in some of them. His youth was spent in a period of rapid and devastating change, and he is neither a victim nor a critic of cultural complexity and sweeping change. He is an adaptive human being who finds that living with the unknown is a norm rather than a threat to his customary lifestyle. Consequently, he can neither understand Dad's fear of the future nor totally sympathize with it. He is the young tiger lurking on the edge of the jungle, teeth bared, eager to flush his first quarry. Dad, on the other hand, is the old mother tiger, scarred from past battles, lying in the sun at the entrance to her den who growls lest the unwary disturb her cub, the business.

Because these two live in different worlds, it is difficult for them to confront mutually the strains which threaten the business. The massive changes in government, technology, communication, and human expectations require the managers of a business to expand their knowledge in a variety of fields in order to cope with the day to day crises of keeping the ship afloat. Law, finance, public relations, regulatory compliance with IRS, OSHA, EEO, EPA,— all have become discrete disciplines requiring professional understanding and competence. It's not a one-truck, one-machine, one-location economy anymore. The son understands this. Dad, on the other hand, fervently hopes it isn't true. He continues to function on the memory of the good old days when all he worried about were customers, and suppliers and competitors, and production.

Technology is developing at such a rapid rate that the knowledge of the average scientist is obsolete within a decade after his graduation. What does that signify for the business owner who has been working on the same management knowledge for 20 to 30 years? It means a search for new markets, new capital, new products—change, growth, hard work. But the founder president is tiring of hard work. He's been there. He's paid his membership. He wants to level off, stabilize the rate of output, and have some opportunity to enjoy the fruits of his labor in these declining years.

ULTIMATE DESTINY—PUBLISH OR PERISH

The argument between father and son cannot continue indefinitely. Either they will discover a happy settlement, or they will destroy the business in their conflict. Time is running out for the business owner. In order to perpetuate the business he has built, he must restructure his concepts. Like the professor seeking tenure in an accredited university, he must publish now, or he will perish.

The problem is that he will die, anyway. But the unknown question is whether it will happen before or after his last landing. And of major concern to his survivors is the fear that he may destroy the airplane. No wonder the aging entrepreneur wakes up in the middle of the night wondering if he is going to survive. So do his passengers, his family and his employees.

Unless he recognizes before it is too late that his main job as president is not to be the best employee his company ever had, but the best teacher of a star student—his successor—then he and his company will go to the grave together. The term "president" for a 55 year old owner of a privately held business has got to be equated with "teacher." And unless he opens up his school, he will not have time to play the graduation march before the requiem sounds.

"GLUE SNIFFING" IN THE EXECUTIVE SUITE

I am convinced from years of working with thousands of owner managers that the myths the president teaches himself are no more than that—myths. The biggest "glue-sniffers" I know are not college students. They are private business owners who sniff their own glue. The myths the owner manager fosters do not represent the truth about himself or the nature of his business. And the first means of providing help is to explode the myths.

1. *His business is not different.* Like the proverbial ostrich who gets shot while hiding his head in the sand, he simply finds it convenient to think so. He can get help. He must first admit to himself that he needs help, that he wants help, and that he will use help.

2. *His experience is not as valid as he thinks it is.* Tenure does not create experience, it fosters only immobility and mildew. He needs to open the windows of his narrow world and let in some light and air . . . to recognize change and the need for new viewpoints on the business.

3. *His money is not his alone.* He can't take it with him into the box, and Uncle Sam will be only one of the inheritors of what he has accumulated. This uncle has unique influence over what will happen to the money. The assets really belong to a lot of people who helped to make its accumulation possible.

4. *His business is not lousy.* It has provided him a successful, respected, comfortable life, and, given the opportunity, he'd do it all over again. In fact, that is part of the problem. He is trying to relive the glory years through instant replay—where he can enjoy the victory without suffering the sweat. Besides, he enjoys the admiration he gets with his self-inflicted injuries, and he likes to tell his kids they're not tough enough, or that the game is too dirty or that he plays with or against bums. If a new quarterback were to get into the game, the business owner would have to do more bench riding than he's willing to do. So instead of turning over the playbook, he mumbles, "Not with my money, you don't."

5. *He did not build the business alone and it is not his to destroy.* Without the support of a loving wife and the understanding of a first class family, great employees, loyal suppliers, and good customers, he might never have made it through the swampy years. Now, safe on firm ground, he must share the bounty with those who stood by him in the marshes.

THE BUCK STOPS HERE—THE FAMILY'S CONCERNS

If he is to provide for the successful continuity of his business, the owner manager must recognize these myths as the illusions which they really are. He can no longer afford the luxury of tilting with windmills, battling false dragons, or creating mountains out of molehills. Business perpetuation is a very real problem which can be solved only by attacking it head on, recognizing its symptoms and its cures, and planning for dealing with its seriousness.

What can he do to provide for the future of his company? I think the answer has two parts: first, he must *maximize his options* as time passes; second, he must accept an *audit of his decisions and actions* for successful survival.

1. *Maximizing the Options*

From the earliest days of his business, the business owner has narrowed the options open to him. Instead of building a management team, instead of taking the time to prepare his heir for succession, instead of finding first rate advisors, instead of developing a useful and competent Board of Directors, instead of using modern accounting techniques to inform his management rather than confuse the IRS, instead of sharing information with and teaching others, he decided he would rather do it all himself. It made him feel vital, virile, heroic. So as his business grew bigger and bigger, he became narrower and narrower and more indispensable. But it may not be too late to reverse the trend. To maximize his options he must share his goals, his dreams, and his actions. He must involve his family, his managers, his employees, his advisors and his directors in the survival of the business instead of doing everything himself and trying to compensate for their inadequacy. The reason they don't understand him or the business is that he never insisted that they learn. Remember who hired them in the first place.

2. *Accepting an Audit of Decisions and Actions*

And, in order to find out how well he is doing at this job of maximizing his options, the owner must provide for periodic monitoring of the system. He needs outside review, badly. He needs people who are knowledgeable, trustworthy, and committed to his goals and to those of his company. He needs people who won't try to con him but who will tell him honestly how they think he is doing in his attempt to maximize his options. People who will not be afraid to press his touchy button, put their finger on his pulse . . . point out his errors as well as his achievements. These kinds of people must be asked to serve as his advisors and as directors on his board.

The business owner who strives to pursue these two steps has already wrestled with his angel and has made his decision. He has decided that his creation is to be a perpetuating business not just a profitable hobby, and he does not intend to kill it by plunder, neglect, or sale. He'll do what has to be done. He knows there is no free lunch.

To assure the survival, the profitable growth, and the successful continuity of his company, the business owner must now begin to effect changes in the five areas of his activity: (1) managing his people (2) managing his money, (3) gaining commitment from outsiders, (4) managing succession (5) managing the estate and sharing the dream, and (6) managing time.

If I were Moses, I would select within these five areas of concern Twelve Commandments for the business owner in search of specifics for his economic salvation:

1. Thou shalt inform thy managers and employees, "This company will continue forever."

2. Thou shalt continue to improve thy management knowledge, that of thy managers and that of thy family.

3. Thou shalt develop a workable organization and make it visible on a chart.

4. Thou shalt institute an orthodox accounting system and make available the data therefrom to thy managers, advisors, and directors.

5. Thou shalt develop a council of competent advisors.

6. Thou shalt submit thyself to the review of a board of competent outside directors.

7. Thou shalt choose thy successor(s).

8. Thou shalt be responsible that thy successor(s) be well taught.

9. Thou shalt retire and install thy successor(s) with thy powers within thy lifetime.

10. Thou canst not take it with thee—so settle thy estate plans—now.

11. Thou shalt share thy dream with thy family.

12. Thou shalt apportion thy time to see that these commandments be kept.

Keep them in mind as you read on.

Chapter Five

Managing People

SUCCESS IS STAYING EMPLOYED

Unfortunately, the family owned company does not have naturally within itself the seeds of its own managerial continuity. Too often no one ever plans for the continuity of the business or feels responsible for its perpetuation.

Consequently there is probably no greater fear or concern among employees of family held businesses than that the owner might throw in the sponge someday, and blame it on the Democrats, governmental intervention, shortages of resources, union influence or big business competition.

Managers in a private company are generally helpless and immobile. They are either too scared to get out and get another job, or they are too old, too timid, or too romanced. They fear that they have been on the same job too long, and their experience is now out of date or irrelevant. Whatever they know, the owner manager has taught them. Their lack of knowledge is often the direct result of the owner's inability to teach them or his own dated learning. These employees are parochial in the sense that they have never been anywhere else. They have always worked for the same people in the same industry—usually, people committed to the status quo. The boss likes things the way they are. He doesn't want to change. So the managers just pray that he knows what he's doing. No wonder they worry when he gets sick.

The definition of success for too many employees in a family owned company is that the plane stay in the air and that they stay employed. They'll never be a private pilot. They don't want to assume the risks of operating their own business. A job change is not a challenge to them. It's a threat. All the president has to do to whip them in line is to threaten to cut off the gas, sell out, or merge.

The owner manager begins to pay the price of piloting his own plane when he recognizes that he has no co-pilot up there in the air with him to whom he can entrust the business. If he goes to Florida for a week, he has to be sure that there is a phone by the pool so that he can run the office long distance. His golf cart is equipped with a walkie-talkie back to the club house, because he's sure the office may need him anytime. He's trapped in the cockpit. Even though he can pay his way out, he can't find anyone who is competent enough to be worth the money and stable enough to accept the accompanying guff.

Why do business owners put up with managers with limited horizons? Because they can't often attract any other kinds, that's why. Look at the typical family business. The owner is about 50-55. His company has bumped along for about 20 years and now, approaching its twentyfifth year, it is riding smoothly and profitably. The owner enjoys the purr of a well tuned engine and the clear view of a fertile, affluent landscape as he flies over it.

Then along comes a bright young fellow of about 30 who wants a seat in the plane; he wants to work in the company. But the more he looks at the prospects, the more he realizes that the owner isn't getting any younger, and the business may not outlast its founder. So this bright young man reasons, "If this guy lives to be 70 and keeps on flying the plane, I'll be 50 when he quits. If this business goes down when he dies, what happens to me? Can I afford to take the chance?" The family business is ruled out by the very ones who want to do the best work. They would rather go where the future does not hinge on one man's immortality.

LOYAL INCOMPETENCE

In family businesses key employees seem to come in at an early age, at menial job levels and remain throughout their working lifetimes in the same company, unless, by some accident they are fired or have the guts to quit. Therefore, these companies seem to harbor an inordinately large number of 45-50 year old employees with 25 years service and 15-20 more years to go who are sidetracked by the boss, frustrated in ambition, too young to retire, and too old to go outside. They have become, in effect, adopted family, and the owner manager is loathe to let them go, even if they have outlived their usefulness. Having them around is comfortable, and they are easily cowed. Their name is Legion, and their continued employment is one of the hidden costs of success.

Such managers long ago accepted somebody else's responsibility for setting goals, long term plans and objectives. If they don't like the way that these goals are implemented, they are resigned to the inevitable. Too seldom are employee managers in a family owned business involved at the policy making level of the business. Their activity is oriented to the present, not the future. Unlike the owner manager, they are not concerned with the total view of the business. The employees make products. The employees sell to customers. The employees add figures.

The difference between the employee and the owner is illustrated by the story of two Irish bricklayers. Somebody asked the first, "What are you doing, Pat?" He answered. "You damn fool, can't you see? I'm laying brick." The same person went over to the other bricklayer, the head contractor and asked him, "What are you doing, Mike?" He replied, "I'm building a cathedral."

The lack of competent managers to challenge the owner president and provide a continuing chain of command into the future is hazardous to the health of a family owned business. For the company to continue, the business owner must be able to attract a management in which he has full confidence. His managers, in turn, must know, understand, and believe his goals. Continued secrecy and non-review of the owner and his policies, his practices and his philosophies can only lead to the ultimate demise of his business.

Solutions to the problems of managing people in the family owned business involve three steps:

1) *assuring* the employees that their company will continue,

2) *reinforcing* this assurance with a continuing program for improving the education of managers, and

3) *developing* a workable organization and making its structure visible.

Although these may appear to be simple steps, they are not accomplished without much thought and effort. They require a commitment of the manager's time, resources, and energy, to be sure that the individual steps are carried out thoroughly and that they achieve the results he intends.

"THIS COMPANY WILL CONTINUE . . ."

If you believe that your business is something that should continue on after you, tell your employees that it is your hope and dream as owner that your business be continued into the future. Post this statement on the bulletin board in big print for everyone to read. Make it known at all levels.

If you can make this kind of statement of faith and purpose, you will go a long way toward solving many of your management problems. It's something like telling your wife that you love her. It shouldn't be implicit; make it explicit. Tell your employees that this business of yours and theirs is going to continue. You will be surprised at the people who will come up to you—the janitor, the sales manager, the inventory clerk, the suppliers. I'll give you odds that two days after you do this, people will come out of the woodwork to tell you how relieved they are to know that their company is going to continue. They want to know that you are going to stay in business and that after you, the enterprise that you created will continue in the image you set for it.

Such a statement has other positive results. The realization that the company will offer work well beyond the lifetime of the owner is a strong motivating factor in recruiting competent young people into the business. If they know that there will be useful work for them to do as they increase their abilities and skills, then young people will consider joining the owner-managed firm with the same confidence that they consider employment in a publicly owned corporation. For older workers, it will be a pledge of assurance that they have given their lives to a worthwhile company, and that the security for which they have struggled all these years will exist in their old age. No longer will they have to worry whether they outlive the business owner. This simple act of confidence, therefore, provides a great service to all of the employees whose work and loyalty have contributed to the growth of the business and the wealth which the owner manager has acquired and enjoyed in his lifetime.

By making it known to his employees, his suppliers, his customers, his community, that he intends to continue his business beyond his working lifetime, the business owner immediately increases his options. He not only eliminates some of the anxiety surrounding the working life of his older employees, but he opens the doors of his firm to talented newcomers who may strengthen his management team. Further, he commits himself to a wide range of changes within his business in order to fulfill this commitment to the future and gives purpose to their implementation. His responsibility for having chosen competent successors installed and in command is now seen as a vital need to the economic well being of all.

IMPROVING KNOWLEDGE AT THE MANAGEMENT LEVEL

One means of convincing the management team that he does, indeed, mean what he says in the words *"This business will continue. . ."* is for the business owner to implement immediately a plan for improving his own management knowledge and that of his key managers and his family. Making an effort to upgrade the skills of all those responsible for the conduct of the business will assure employees far more than will lengthy documents that the business owner is investing in the continuity of his business.

Just as a business which isn't designed to make a profit doesn't last long, so a business that is not committed to the continuing education of its key personnel is not preparing itself for a bright future. The business owner must spend some of his company's time, money and energies not only on the management education of the boss but also on the management education of his advisors, directors, managers, and family. Although the benefits of this education may not show quickly in the profit statement, they most certainly will eventually.

There is no purpose in concentrating all of the education around the boss. He goes to all the seminars because they are held in Acapulco, and he gets smarter and smarter while the "help" stays home. Because they are standing still rather than progressing at the same rate as the business owner, he thinks they are getting dumber and dumber. No wonder they don't understand; he doesn't make it possible for them to learn. The purpose of business education is to bring others up to the point where they can share in the problems of the chief executive. Education is never free. It costs money; it costs time; it sometimes even costs some faith. The participants in a family business cannot educate themselves without the support and commitment of the owner to their desire for increased understanding and his promise not to waste their learning. The first person to understand the need for management development, which is, essentially, self-development, should be the head man, the boss. His need is to help educate everybody else who wants to learn. I have yet to find someone whose talents could not be improved. If the business owner makes a major attempt to help his people recognize that the enlargement of their business understanding is something that the company will invest its time and money in, he will be amazed at the additional commitment that people at all levels will make in the company's future. The business owner and I are in the same business—we both run schools—we are both teachers. But too often he doesn't recognize it.

THE ENTREPRENEURIAL UNIVERSITY

Many business owners, unfortunately, turn a deaf ear to the suggestion that they need to spend more time educating themselves and their management team. Having been burned once by a bad seminar or a meeting which proved to be a waste of time, they vow never to spend another penny on such "foolhardiness." It is too bad that they treat education this way. If one of their customers returned a product that proved defective and claimed that all such products were defective, they would take offense, and rightly so. Similar problems occur in education. There are useful and worthwhile educational programs and there are those which waste the time of the owner and demean his position. Just as no competent business-man would buy a product without checking its value, neither should he purchase educational services without investigating the reputation of the educator and the benefits of the program.

How does the owner manager who really wants to improve his own education and that of his managers accomplish this task? There are many levels of management programs run by institutes, universities, and associations. Since the thrust and emphasis of those programs will vary in value from sponsor to sponsor, it is wise to contact the specific educational institution about its program: the purpose, the content, the faculty, and previous experience in the field. Careful weighing of this vital material will enable the owner manager to invest his education dollars in a useful, professional program geared specifically to his needs as a private business owner.

If the owner manager remembers that too many of those who educate the professional manager of a publicly owned corporation may have no understanding of the needs of the family owned and privately held business, he will be less likely to enroll in a course which does not meet his specific needs. In checking out the validity of the program, it would be wise for him to ask such questions as

- "How long have you been working with owner managers?"

- "What is your reputation in your field?"

- "Is your thrust attuned to both the problems and resources of the private business owner, or is this program a fill-in for idle periods in an institution really geared to turning out managers for conglomerates?"

- "Are faculty members experienced in dealing with the problems of the owner managed business?"

- "Do they understand the conflicts which can occur between business goals and family goals?"

- "What have been your results in the past?"

Answers to these and similar questions will help the business owner locate educational programs designed to meet his needs.

All seminars should provide both an opportunity for skilled teachers to offer necessary knowledge effectively and at the lowest cost in time and money to those who need help, as well as a forum wherein the business owner/participant can find such help without feeling that such requests for information or assistance reflect upon his ability, his virility, or his immortality as a divine provider.

From long experience, conducting educational programs, I feel strongly that when the boss goes to seminars, workshops or conferences, he should not go alone. He should take someone with him with whom he can discuss the subject matter on his return, with whom he can expand upon the concepts developed. This is a vital ingredient in his own commitment to audit his decisions and actions, for it provides a sounding board for the kind of "action plan" he develops as a result of his attendance. Similarly, when he sends his management team or his successors, the boss should not send them alone. At least a pair group of peers should attend educational programs together.

Husbands and wives make good pairs to go to programs of philosophic content on the ultimate direction and design of their business goals. Fathers and sons make good pairs to attend programs involving the training of the successor for developing future corporate management plans and policies. Brothers make good pairs to attend programs in which the pressures, problems, and priorities inherent in management development and management control and management succession in the family business need to be understood by both. Sometimes the wives of these young men need to attend the programs with their husbands so that when the problems in the future structure of the business become more emotional and more knotty, a framework already exists to help these ambitious young ladies understand, accept and participate in the decisions of their husbands in the continuing journey of the family business.

Going alone to an educational experience is like going to the movies by yourself and then going home and trying to explain the picture to your wife. No matter how articulate you may be, some of the best and most meaningful parts leave you incapable of explaining them. You end up by saying, "You should have been there." The experience of a seminar has no TV replays. The business owner cannot afford to make the mistake of the movie-goer when he schedules participation in seminars for himself, his family, his advisors, his managers. It is far better for the boss to go to half as many programs and to take along another participant who can learn with him than it is for him to go to twice as many seminars and carry away only half of the content, because he had no sympathetic partner with whom to share his information.

PROVIDING EDUCATION IS USEFUL HELP

Good sources of continuing education for business owners and their managers which should not be overlooked are the increasing number of programs offered for their distributors by concerned manufacturers and the seminars sponsored by trade and professional associations involved with the owner-manager. More manufacturers who are dependent upon privately owned distributors and suppliers would do well to create such management seminars and encourage participation by the business owner, his managers and his successors. Helping them plan their future more professionally should be of vital concern to the manufacturer since the potential demise of any distributor can jeopardize the very future of the manufacturer.

As one enlightened big company sales manager said to me, "We have no choice but to help our distributors to keep their businesses profitable, stable, healthy and growing through the years to come. It is no longer sufficient for any manufacturer to limit its help to 'product and application' information. To survive and grow, successful manufacturers must do everything possible to help upgrade the continuing management skills of their distributors." Or as another wise old vice president of sales once told me, "You can't shear a dead sheep but once."

Here again is an area in which banks, insurance companies, and public accounting firms—to name but a few of all those who should have an interest in keeping entrepreneurship alive—can become involved. A seminar is an opportunity to educate the private business owner at the lowest possible cost for the maximum benefit both to the sponsor in its search for relevant new purpose and profitable new directions, and to the participant in search of answers to new problems.

As just one example, let us look at the opportunity present for trade and professional associations to explore and then develop areas in which—as the new "University of the Entrepreneur"—they can contribute increasingly to the well being and progress of their members. An association cannot simply frustrate its membership by diagnosing without prescribing. Any association which merely takes up the time of its members is not filling its member's needs. It must help the member to invest his time with the association to the member's advantage. Membership in an association must mean not merely participation in a vehicle that asks for the investment of money; an association must be a vehicle in which all participants can invest their time. It must be a vehicle in which participants can invest their dreams and hopes for accomplishments that exceed their ability alone. Somehow, it must, by its efforts, find ways of rewarding its participants with more time through education. It must play a dominant role in their lives and offer very special rewards for participation and commitment.

An association must help the business owner understand and establish his priorities in solving his multiple concerns:

- His ever-increasing needs for more professionalism as an employee

- Better organization as a manager

- Safety of investment as an owner

- Enjoyment and purpose as a successful man

In this way, the association can become the entrepreneur's economic university, his business temple.

The curriculum of such an association program must be designed for a continuing journey and must take into account the differing needs of man in the different stages of his life. What, in fact, can the association do for this man as part of its curriculum? Too many association members seem not to know nor to care what their organization does for them in providing services and programs. Why? Because too many associations act like the proverbial mousetrap manufacturer who feels the world would or should beat a path to his door.

Teachers who have found success in the field of adult continuing education have discovered that the biggest factor in making any program a success is in convincing the student of the value of the class and developing his desire to continue in it. The association can emulate this philosophy by making programs meaningful and relevant to members' needs and by communicating this need to its members with enthusiasm. The programs and the curriculum must be designed by age and career requirements, by organizational size, and by ownership and management interests. Thus, they can be designed for a homogeneous group with definable and specific goals, needs and abilities.

For instance, as the individual starts his career as a young man, he has all of the challenges of the future ahead of him. He needs help in preparing for these challenges, through programs which continue his formal education and enlarge his horizons and which point up the excitement of participation in an ever-changing environment. He should be helped to see how he can contribute to society. Who better than his association can offer him a voice in translating his ideas into reality?

As an emerging manager, a man needs guidelines for organizing his time, his resources, his subordinates, and his goals into a meaningful plan for successful operation. Who better than an association can marshall the data, the specialists, the resources necessary to upgrade managerial skills to assist a man in coping with his growing responsibilities and to understand better his role in a complex and changing socio-political and economic climate?

As fathers, men are concerned with their son's understanding and acceptance of their world. It has been only recently that a man wondered whether his son would follow his career. Dad's business is no longer necessarily the first choice of the young.

As a husband, the entrepreneur or manager needs to have his wife understand the conflicts in value judgments and the continuing tradeoffs that he must accept each day in the course of his business or professional responsibility. The husband is absorbed by problems his wife doesn't understand. He seeks goals she doesn't necessarily accept. What better response can an organization make to these needs than by structuring its annual meetings to include meaningful educational programs for wives rather than the usual bridge games, shopping tours and fashion shows and other forms of deductible baby sitting?

Finally, as men approach that pinnacle of economic success which represents the end of the journey, most realize that they can't take it with them; (not all of them, of course, but most.) An enlightened association can assist in a field of need which is immense; estate planning, retirement planning, management development, ownership transferral, executive succession, income continuance plans, investment planning for the protection of the family interests. It is an endless and vitally important list. At this stage of life these are urgent problems. If any association does not accept the responsibility of preserving the footprints that its members have made on the sands of time, then it must share with them the responsibility for the disappearance of their precious ingredient of success, a commitment to the future.

The business owner on the other hand, must not frustrate associations in their attempt to supplement his education. He should be a dedicated student in a vital program and encourage his managers and family to become involved in such programs. Education of the business family is not a "once in a lifetime" thing. It must be part of the continuing journey of the business owner and he should embrace all opportunities available to him and his management to learn. These opportunities are all too rare and the need for them are ever growing.

For example, in the hope of partially meeting this need at our own Institute, we annually sponsor three different kinds of programs.

1. *For business owners and their key men*: intensive 2½ day seminars designed for active participation by chief executive officers

and their # 1 managers, and/or their potential successors, to help them identify and solve the problems of their own business. The seminars are not lecture courses. Workshop topics covered include such subjects as: "Financing Continuity;" "Separating Personal and Corporate Goals;" "Management Development for Succession and Continuity;" "Utilizing Advisors and Directors;" "Using Accounting and Financial Data;" "Establishing Effective Management Controls;" "Income & Estate Planning." Their effectiveness is in getting modern management thinking in a number of areas not readily available to most business owners.

    2. *For business owners and their wives*: week long invitational seminars held at quiet and secluded resorts to provide for leisurely yet wide-ranging exploration by participating husbands and wives who "follow the dream" of a vigorous, perpetuating, family owned business. The seminars are designed to help the decision makers in the family owned business talk with each other about business planning. Where, heretofore, there was either reluctance, no time, or no forum for such understanding and exchange, these programs provide each couple an opportunity to explore together the organization of their family firm, plans for their estate, and the problems of managing their money, managing their people, and managing their business for the successful continuity of their company.

    3. *For the young heirs of business owners*: three day conferences for young men and women between the ages of 17-25 who face the decision of planning their future in the family owned business. The conference stresses frank and open discussion of such topics as "What's It Like, Running Your Own Business?" "Is Your Business His Business?" "Life with Father, Compared to What?" "A Company President Look At His Job," "Does A Family Business Do Its Share?" With a faculty of articulate business owner/fathers who "tell it like it is," these conferences aim at exposing the young to the facts of business life, its risks and its rewards, its limitations and its satisfactions in offering a lifestyle of contribution to both family and society.

    All Institute programs are staffed by professionals vitally interested in the survival of the family owned business—men who have worked closely within a variety of family companies and have been widely exposed to the power structure of these companies and the resulting problems. Bankers, lawyers, accountants, psychologists, consultants, and other specialists with national reputations in the field of the owner managed business, address themselves to the corporate and management practices of the family owned business. All programs are planned to provide maximum learning within an optimum use of the business owner's prime resource—time. For over a decade now, these seminars have attracted national acclaim for their ability to draw participants from a wide spectrum of successful family companies, who share their knowledge with their peers and successors in an open forum of frank, down-to-earth discussion.

GROWING ORGANIZATIONAL STRUCTURES NEED ORGANIZATION CHARTS

The typical businessman only learns how to acquire, not to share. He learns how to work, but not teach. He learns how to solve some problems, but not how to ask for help from others when he faces problems which he can't solve. As he increases his management education, he will begin to accept the fact that most of his problems are of his own design. The first and foremost problem, really, is himself. His whole relationship to the business has been that of technician, not manager, and the change of attitude and behavior which he must effect in order to become a first rate manager can be a painful awakening.

But he is certainly not alone in his plight. Most managers enter the owner-managed enterprise with less management knowledge than the boss, and, unless he supports their continued education, they don't gain too much knowledge on the job beyond a parochial view of the work they are doing. Neither the boss nor the help have ever been managers before. They have no objective criteria for judging their performance or charting their development as the company grows, when they should be growing, too. Employees, especially, find such an atmosphere difficult because they have no way of knowing whether their job performance is good, bad, or indifferent. All they know is that they haven't been fired. It's a little like assuming that they have happy marriages because their wives haven't left them.

Objective assessment of performance in the family owned business is frequently difficult because the owner has never instituted a clearly defined organizational structure and made it visible on an organizational chart; he has not written job descriptions for all positions; he has not developed a regular system of performance review for all employees. Instead he capriciously hands out titles or raises when he feels good, and declares periodic bonuses if the company shows a higher than expected pretax profit.

Taking time to educate his key employees to become better managers is a wasted investment, however, unless the business owner also develops an organizational structure to support these more competent managers. The technical means of illustrating such a structure is through an organization chart. One of the reasons that an organization chart is essential is that it provides a means for separating corporate and personal relationships. Family owned businesses suffer from their early needs for cheap personnel when the owner recruited the only employees likely to work the long hours at low pay, his friends and relatives. Years later these same people are often still around, but their contribution was usually most helpful where and when they came in at the entry level. They did not really have, nor have they usually gained any professional management competence. As the business grew, the organization became a conflicting mixture of family and outsiders. The family may be the toughest group to handle. In addition to being employees, these people often are shareholders. How do you handle an incompetent family-employee-shareholder?

Most businesses can afford a couple of family pets. What they can't afford is a couple of family pets who try to earn their keep. If the owner wants to take his wife's maiden sister and keep her on the payroll as the bookkeeper, it would be cheaper to just send her a check. He shouldn't allow her to obstruct his accounting department by her attempt to monitor the system. Or if Uncle Charlie can't get work elsewhere after fifteen years in his nephew's nuts and bolts factory, then the nephew should make him branch manager in charge of the Siberian office. He can be kept on as a philanthropic activity supported 50% by the government as a business expense because his keep is written off as salary but no business owner can run a company by maintaining pets in vital structures. The non-productive family member really has no place in the business. An organizational chart, honestly drawn, may help to solve this problem.

WHAT DOES THE COMPANY LOOK LIKE . . . ON PAPER?

An organization chart should be like a map, a flight plan, or a diagram for the professional football player. It tells a manager where he is, where he has come from, where it is possible for him to progress, and who is there to help him. Just as a professional manager can't keep books on the back of an envelope, he can't keep an organization chart in his head. Those who do usually find that they are out of date. Some people have quit. Some have died. Some have been fired. The company may have been reorganized. The fact is that few owner managers could produce an organization chart if asked to do so, and, even if they could, not too many could produce one which has been updated in the last six months.

An organization chart provides the business owner with a visible tool for auditing his decisions and actions in the area of administration and personnel. Further, it offers his key managers a similar tool for reviewing their growth and the development of the company. The organization chart provides a mechanism for indicating the lines of command within the business. It shows 1) who is, or is supposed to be, responsible for what; 2) to whom that person is immediately responsible at the job level above him; 3) to whom he can look for support below him (including the delegation of some tasks and responsibilities), and 4) to which position he has access in his upward mobility within the company as he gains experience and status within the organization.

The organization chart offers another means of motivating employees. Most motivational literature has been written for managers of publicly held companies where opportunities for stock options, advancement, divisional transfers, and various other gimmicks are available as supplementary motivational forces. Little has been written about motivation in the privately held company because the successful entrepreneur who may be a prime motivator is not usually an author. The reason good men want to work for privately held firms at the management level is so that they can be closer to the action; so that they can see the results of their work; so that they can witness the immediate cause-and-effect relationship of their efforts. Show them a clearly drawn organization chart that positively reinforces their sense of participation in the success of the company. What better way to motivate a man than to show him how he shares in some of the rewards he helped to create not only through increased compensation, but also through upward mobility, job enrichment, self fulfillment and a sense of participation. Let him see it objectively.

LOCATING WINNERS AND LOSERS

An organization chart for the privately held company should contain in proper descending order the shareholders, directors, officers, managers, and supervisory personnel. (See Figure 6) It need not go down to the level of productive labor nor include the girls in the steno pool. In addition the chart should indicate how the outside advisors affect the functions in various departments of the business. Since most family owned companies do not employ full time legal departments and some not even full time accounting departments, the lawyer or accountant that works on a retainer basis actually fills that slot. Not to include him on the organization chart would be confusing, because his participation in the company has strong managerial overtones.

An organization chart is not very useful unless it is kept current, and unless its contents are made known to the management group. If the warehouse superintendent leaves, his name should be eliminated from the chart and that of his replacement should be entered. If the superintendent's leaving caused management shifts elsewhere in the structure, then they also should be noted.

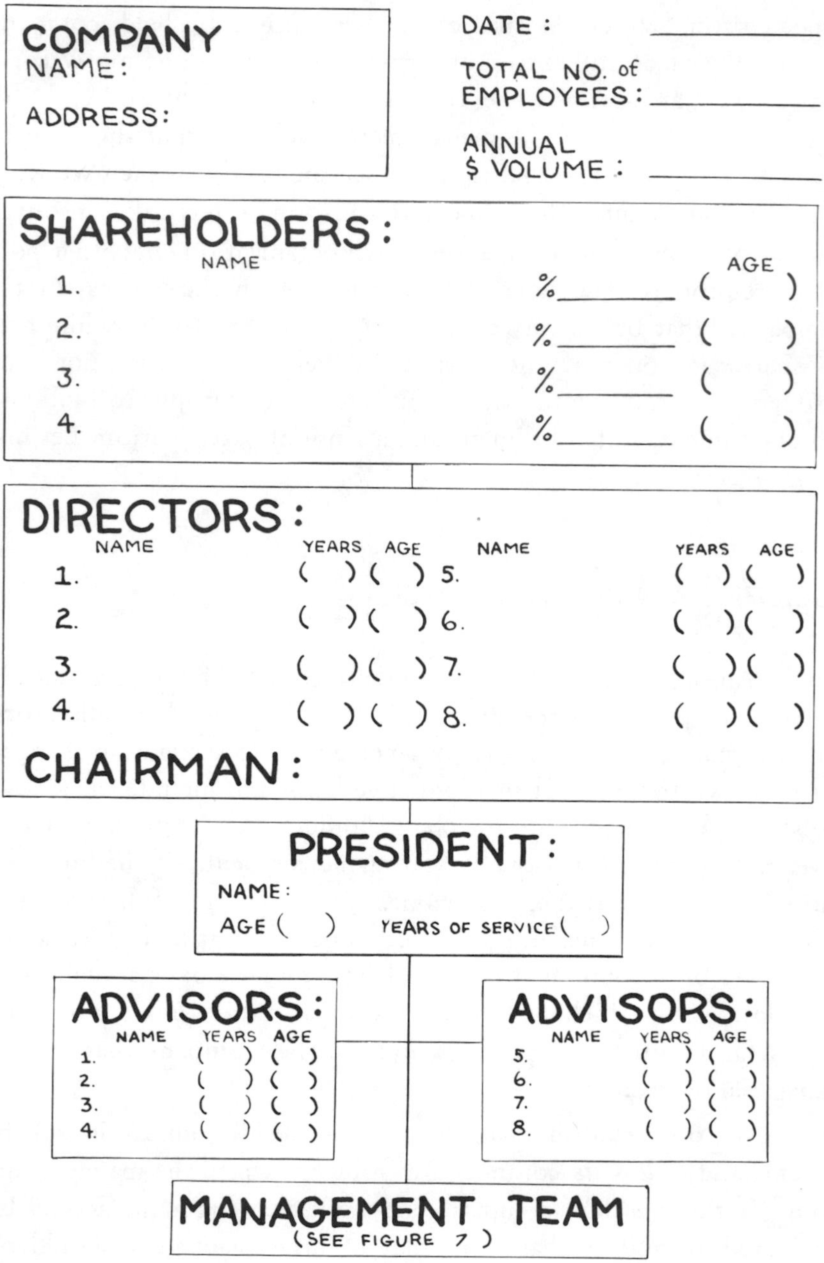

COMPANY
NAME:

ADDRESS:

DATE : _____

TOTAL NO. of
EMPLOYEES : _____

ANNUAL
$ VOLUME : _____

SHAREHOLDERS :

NAME   AGE
1.   %_____ (   )
2.   %_____ (   )
3.   %_____ (   )
4.   %_____ (   )

DIRECTORS :

NAME	YEARS AGE	NAME	YEARS AGE
1.	( ) ( )	5.	( ) ( )
2.	( ) ( )	6.	( ) ( )
3.	( ) ( )	7.	( ) ( )
4.	( ) ( )	8.	( ) ( )

CHAIRMAN :

PRESIDENT :
NAME:
AGE (   )   YEARS OF SERVICE (   )

ADVISORS :

NAME	YEARS AGE
1.	( ) ( )
2.	( ) ( )
3.	( ) ( )
4.	( ) ( )

ADVISORS :

NAME	YEARS AGE
5.	( ) ( )
6.	( ) ( )
7.	( ) ( )
8.	( ) ( )

MANAGEMENT TEAM
(SEE FIGURE 7)

Figure 6.

ORGANIZATION CHART

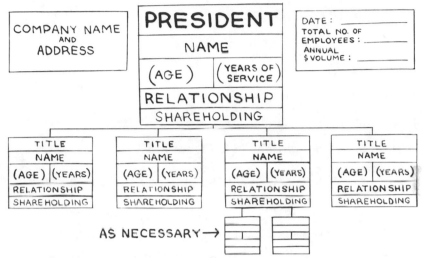

DON'T FORGET TO PUT IN:

* ALL VICE-PRESIDENTS
* THE TREASURER
* THE SECRETARY
* ALL MANAGERS/DIRECTORS of DEPARTMENTS
* ALL THE RELATIVES AND INVESTORS : FATHER, MOTHER - UNCLES IN-LAWS - NEPHEWS PARTNER'S FAMILY- THE DENTIST
  ON THE PAYROLL (EVEN THOSE WITHOUT JOBS!)

AND THEN PREPARE:

* A GOOD JOB DESCRIPTION FOR EVERY JOB
* A GOOD RESUME FOR EVERY MANAGER
* A SALARY HISTORY FOR EVERY MANAGER
* MAYBE EVEN AN EVALUATION of POTENTIAL!

FOR EVERY MANAGEMENT JOB AND JOB HOLDER.

Figure 7.

Make the chart truly informative. Each management position should have an individual square. Divide the square into six sections:

(a)   *title* of the position

(b)   the *name* of the person occupying the position

(c)   the *age* of that person

(d)   *his number of years of service* with the company,

(e)   *his shareholdings*, and

(f)   *his family relationship.* (See Figure 7)

If you really want a shock—put down salaries, bonuses and fringes in a box next to each position.

The result of this exercise is always astounding. The business owner quickly discovers how few people in his organization really know anything objectively because the only place they've ever worked is in his firm, and he has never taken the time to teach them anything new or explain to them how the company really functions. Most of the employees have been there almost as long as the owner, and what little they've learned, they learned from him. The need for fresh air and fresh thought is obvious. For real perspective, the business owner might try drawing this same chart as it appeared five years ago and ten years ago. It's most revealing for it substantiates the lack of real personnel growth in the company.

For instance, the business owner should investigate how much movement there has been in key positions in the past twenty years. Is the sales manager the same man who handled the job when the company began? If not, where is he now, up, down, or sideways in the organization? Has his area of responsibility grown, diminished or remained the same? What is his competence? What about his compensation? Is it based on loyalty, tenure, or ability? If essentially the same people exist in the same positions but are just making more money, then the owner doesn't have a management team. He may just have a bunch of hangers-on whose only hope is that *he* outlives *them.* In order to get new blood into the firm before it's too late, he may have to take radical steps to reorganize, retire, or pension off the old guard so that a new guard can move up. Who should go out, and when? Who should move up? Who needs more or different responsibility? The chart may help to determine all this. But don't dodge the issues.

At some point in the architecture of the chart the winners and losers will begin to stand out. The flaws in the owner's personal judgment will become apparent. So will his accurate decisions. If continuity is his goal, therefore, and he assumes that the firm is going to grow over the next ten years, he'll begin to audit the personnel decisions he has made as they are graphically illustrated by the chart. He'll take a hard look at who will be there ten years, twenty years from now to continue the business. Unless the business owner plans now to educate them for a productive future, they will not be any smarter in ten years, just older. Age is a mathematical proposition, a fact. Whether a company prepares for it or not, people do get older. With training, they also get smarter.

Another thing which usually becomes apparent in such a chart is that the company has grown over the past 10-20 years. In all probability that growth has been accompanied by increased complexity. No one will deny that life is more complex today than it was 20 years ago, even 10 and 5 years ago, as the logistics, requirements, and amounts of technical and non-technical knowledge increase. The organization chart should reflect the increased complexity of the business. For alert business owners such indicators quickly propel them into checking whether they have kept pace with the growing complexity of their business, by preparing and staffing for additional requirements or opportunities. In some sad cases, the business has grown beyond the owner; it has really passed him by, and he remains a relic of the glory of the early days.

ORGANIZATION CHARTS ILLUSTRATE PROBLEMS

Some of the confusion which can occur when a company operates on the basis of a faulty organization is illustrated by the examples charted below. Obviously these are not the real names of the businesses whose charts are reproduced, but they were actually drawn by officers of real companies who diagramed the operation within their companies for me.

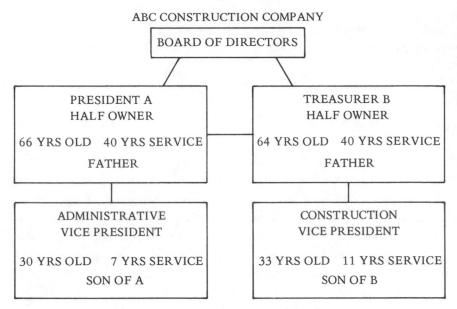

Figure 8.

The chart for the ABC Company (Figure 8) would indicate that the firm is administered jointly by the president and the treasurer who own equal shares. Both report to the board of directors, which is composed of the two "partner" owners, and their two sons. In effect, the executive officers report to themselves and their progeny. Obviously such an arrangement does not provide a very real kind of review over a volatile administrative situation.

The organization chart reflects the problems which occurred in the formation of the business. The company started as a partnership. In forming the corporation, the older of the partners became president and the younger became executive vice president and treasurer. The younger partner, however, never accepted a subordinate position. Consequently, he has made the position of E.V.P. and Treasurer one of co-presidency. To accommodate this awkward arrangement, the business was carved down the middle. The "treasurer" partner—who never did like finance—assumed responsibility for estimating and the field, the construction end of the business. The "president" partner, who was the extrovert salesman and wheeler-dealer, became the boss of "sales and finance." The

division of labor and responsibilities virtually resulted in accom-
modating two firms under one roof, a finance and marketing concern
and a field construction firm. The two organizations probably could
have managed equally well as two separate organizational entities
providing services and customers to each other. Because the two
partners had created the vehicle to accommodate their preferences,
they found a means of functioning despite the division of the
business and the company has managed to grow reasonably well in
this double harness arrangement. The problems which are beginning
to occur result from the need to pass the torch on to the successive
management. The sons already recognize the problem which will
occur as internal political jockeying is becoming frenzied, particularly among the young wives.

The partners only delayed the real problem of dealing with
organizational structure in setting up this unorthodox co-president
arrangement. If one of them dies before the plans are made for filling
the position of president from the potential successors, the slot may
be filled by default, the surviving partner acting as a strong supporter
of his own son for the job. Promising outside talent would find this
situation frought with tension. Since each line organization exists at
the will of the "partner" president in charge, the loyalties of
management workers are not in this period of ferment directed to
the whole company but rather to that portion of the company in
which they are employed. Any ambitious young man would
recognize that his future depended as much upon the political
maneuvering for top position as it does upon his own competence.
Few people who really want to grow with an organization would find
this an inviting possibility.

The situation in the XYZ Equipment Company (Figure 9) is
a textbook case of "the rake" organization at work. The ownership
of the stock is divided among 5 family members all of whom are
represented on the Board of Directors and all of whom are employed
in the company in positions subsidiary to that of president. In
addition, the management level includes a non-family member who
has no holdings. Considering his age and years of service in relation
to that of the family members on the management staff, this man
can question his future with the company.

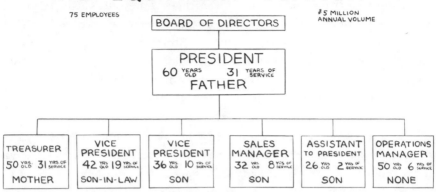

Figure 9.

Old Dad is reaching that time when he is considering taking it easier—semi-retirement. The company faces the classic situation in which all sons are younger and with fewer years of service than a brother-in-law. Who will be elevated to the presidency? What is the relative contribution or responsibility of the positions of the two vice presidents, the treasurer, the sales manager and a general manager? Mother has been active in money management and accounting since the inception and doles out data to no one, least of all to the general manager. She has no intention of quitting her job. She loves the power of being in the middle. All positions are equal because all report directly to Dad and all are on "the Board." There is no chain of command in this company, and no delegation of responsibility from one member of the "team" to another. Dad is the general, Mom is the adjutant, and everyone else is a "private." Redesigning such an organization is difficult only because neither the owner nor his wife really wants to let go of any part of the policy-making or decision-making process. A chart won't solve problems, but it will certainly highlight the problems and put needed actions into some priority. It will also offer an objective view of the company to competent advisors; for their suggestions and help.

The president who looks carefully at his chart and checks his own progress in relationship to the progress of the company will find the organization chart a helpful tool for implementing his new understanding of his role as president. He will recognize that he must, indeed, devote the largest portion of his time to providing for the continuity of his business. He will understand the importance of recruiting and retaining able young employees and will invest time and money in their education. And he will begin to straighten out the kinks in his personnel management by instituting such useful personnel controls as job descriptions and periodic review.

WHO DOES WHAT AND WHEN?

Job descriptions are written to clarify for each manager the tasks he is expected to perform, the degree of authority and responsibilities which he has within the organizational pyramid, and the person to whom he is accountable for the proper performance of his work, and the expectations which the company has for him. They will assist the Boss in allocating his own energies more efficiently. A clearly written job description to which the manager and his Boss can refer at regular periods (6-12 months) is a great step forward in planning for the responsibilities of the future.

A good job description should indicate title, salary range, pre-qualifications for the job and the criteria for promotion, an outline of responsibilities, an indication of those tasks which may be delegated down, and a clear indication of the title holder's boss.

A careful look at job descriptions and an attempt to match them with the people on the organization chart usually indicates to the business owner that (1) the people now occupying the positions may not have the qualifications to fit their responsibilities, or (2) the owner may actually not have given them the responsibility for the job and the authority which goes with it, or (3) he may not have permitted the right to delegate work down the line. In far too many companies the owner has simply aped other structures he has seen, given fancy titles to tedious labor and filled the slots with loyal incompetents.

Unless the owner manager can honestly say that he has filled the positions with the best people he can hire from within his family or outside and really given them the authority that goes with their responsibility, then he is not preparing or developing a management team which can handle the business when he leaves it. Management development means exactly what the words imply, preparing others to take on specific tasks so that when the incumbent is no longer around to perform them, someone else is available and willing to do them. It is not enough to hope that Providence will provide a candidate at the needed time. The substitute must be on deck and functioning, now. If the owner is honestly concerned with developing a competent management team, he will begin at once to clean out the deadwood. He will match job descriptions with organizational chart positions and fill these slots with people who really have the prescribed skills and abilities. If this means reordering the work of family members, he must face that unpleasant task as one of the costs of continuity. "Family pets" have no job descriptions.

In family owned companies, the work of writing job descriptions becomes the unpleasant task of sorting out work relationships and family relationships. As the business owner begins to list titles which require descriptions, he often notices a mixture of family titles (son, son-in-law, brother) covered by "assistant to the president" as a euphemism with occupational titles (plant superintendent, chief engineer, sales manager, purchasing manager). Only the latter are genuine job titles. The former really indicate the manner of entry into the company through family roads.

Sorting out this confusion of titles can be a difficult task. How does the owner tell a brother-in-law that his relationship to the president's wife does not qualify him to be a vice-president? How does he tell a son that his mother is not permitted to promote him over the sales vice president hired from outside?

The subject of wives in the family business is a sticky one. Wives seem to fall into four categories: 1) those who really are involved in the operation of the business; 2) those who are "involved" just so that a title can be filled and not given to someone else or so that the boss can take them on trips and write them off as an officer; 3) those who are really uninvolved and, maybe, don't care to be involved, and 4) those who would like to be involved, but who are not really invited to become involved.

Obviously, there are many cases which come to mind in which a man's wife is actually as competent and responsible in her own right for the development of the business as is her husband. She probably understands the business as well as he, but her involvement, just as the involvement of the non-working wife in the business, changes the complexion of the business in subtle ways. Outsiders often hesitate to challenge, take issue with, or otherwise embarrass a man in front of his wife, especially if she takes an active part in the management of the company.

Usually the wife's job is in the accounting, personnel, or administrative end of the business. In too many cases this provides a mined battlefield between Mom and Dad and the working Son. The Son invariably approaches Mom for understanding of his money needs or goals, just as he used to go to Dad for his allowance. In his struggle to succeed in the business, the relationship is always that of Mother-Son, never controller-manager. Dad gets trapped in the middle, and God help "The Help."

This presents a pretty hard problem to solve. How does the owner replace someone who has additional insights into the job because she is a member of the family as well as a competent employee? Often, he can't, unless he wants to get another wife and give her the same job. It is pretty difficult to replace a Wife-Treasurer. Treasurers can be replaced, but Wife-Treasurers are unique to the family business. Their early contribution may even have made it possible for the business to grow. But most Wife-Treasurers should learn to get out of the business voluntarily as early as possible to avoid inhibiting the kids, alienating the help, frustrating father and fouling up the business full time, from behind their Yalu River.

Writing clear job descriptions, and making it work on a chart provides a company president not only a method for auditing his past decisions, but by focusing in on the confusion between family and job titles, it also offers him a means of maximizing his options. It removes much "secrecy" and clears up much confusion. It opens up the possibility of advancement within the organization to a wider range of competent personnel. If he delegates the authority to the person that the description indicates, he is functioning as a teacher of willing students rather than as a dictator to frightened hirelings. The payoff from this activity can be tremendous. Let me use an example or two.

I was once approached by a buyer who was considering the purchase of a family company, which operated a fleet of produce hauling trucks. The founder was an old man well into his seventies, and both of his sons had opted for other careers. In seeking to establish a value for the purchase of the company, the potential buyer had discovered a confusing array of oldsters in top management positions and the treasurer of the firm was the owner's younger sister, age 50. (Not only was she reluctant to divulge information, she gave strong indications that purchase of the company included purchase of her as an employee since her brother had hired her for life.) The potential buyer asked me what he should do. I suggested that before he bought, he look beyond the treasurer's office to other employees in the company. How many of them were family who had lifetime job guarantees? Was the buyer ready to confront the gravity of a situation in which he might well have to replace a majority of his "management?" Was he in a position to take the anger of the family and the misunderstanding of his customers, if he did decide to make such a clean sweep? Armed with these insights he made a much more thorough investigation of the company he planned to buy, the power structure of the family and the confusion between personal and corporate goals. Convinced that the company was not a viable structure, he lost any interest in acquisition. Eventually after several potential buyers all came to the same conclusion, the same man who had created this inflexible organization finally just liquidated his holdings, and his relatives were left holding an empty bag.

In another instance, I knew a company in which the chief executive office was "shared" by two brothers who had inherited equal ownership. When I asked them both at our first meeting to draw an organization chart of the business for me as they each saw it, the younger brother drew a chart in which he and his brother were both at the top as equals, and the older brother left the younger off his chart entirely. The two brothers had well described their problem.

When I brought out the two charts both brothers exclaimed, "Why hell, we don't really work in the same company!" They were right. The root of the corporate problem was a personal rivalry between the brothers which had existed from early childhood. Many solutions were possible, and these were, fortunately, wise men. The brothers recognized that to undo the behavior of a lifetime might exert undo financial and psychological strain on the company. Eventually, they worked out an agreement which provided a spin off of products, facilities and funds for the younger brother to have an autonomous non-competing, company of his own. That was several years ago. I recently visited both thriving businesses, and I was pleased to find that one of the first things both had done after the spin off was to publish a corporate organization chart which clearly defined the operation of the company. Among other things it contained complete job descriptions for all positions. Both were quick to point out to me that the charts had helped them to avoid some of the mistakes their father had made in substituting fancy job titles for adequate income. Both have been able to attract first rate non-family help. And freed of the intra-family conflict, both companies are on firm ground and will provide a worthwhile inheritance for the generation coming up.

As these examples indicate, the business owner seeking business continuity may face unpleasant circumstances, if he recognizes that his company structure is no longer adequate to do the job. He may even have to plan to replace family members with more competent personnel. These are difficult changes to make, and the power structure of the family will militate against it. But the responsible business owner cannot leave these decisions to his successor. Once he recognizes where the deadwood lies, eliminating it is his job.

Fortunately, if the going gets really rough, he does not have to make the final choices alone. There are industrial psychologists, trainers, and management development consultants, who can help the business owner examine his company structure, evaluate his present personnel, make recommendations for changes, write adequate job descriptions, and design programs for preparing the old guard for retirement or replacement and readying the younger managers for new assignments and more responsibility. To such professionals these problems are not unique. They have performed similar tasks for hundreds of firms. They are equipped to assist the business owner in these personnel areas where he feels uncomfortable, ignorant, or just plain scared.

Chapter Six

Managing Money

THE NAME OF THE GAME IS PROFIT

Few family owned businesses have adequate internal accounting systems, and the outside auditing controls usually aren't much,
either. I have often made the statement that if it were not for the
Internal Revenue Service, most owner managed businesses would go
out of business. I get booed pretty badly at those times, but I still
believe that statement to be essentially true. I am not saying that the
IRS is the saviour of free enterprise, but I do think that the IRS
offers willing students a pretty good education at old IRSU.

The tuition at IRSU is high, but old IRSU makes the business
owner keep books. It forces him to keep track of how much goes in
and how much goes out and what for and to whom. If he doesn't
keep track of all of this in a pretty orthodox way, he loses money or
gets sent to jail. The serious students, on the other hand, make great
contributions to their business. They are the people who use
orthodox accounting systems, first class advisors and competent

insiders, keep good records, and provide a steady flow of financial information to those who need sound data in order to make profitable mangement decisions at all levels.

A well-organized management team can neither direct, nor advise, nor function profitably without the necessary information about the business provided by such a well-designed accounting system. An owner manager who is still functioning with the same accounting practices and personnel he adopted when he founded the business must review and revise his accounting system as the business grows, in order to assure himself that he is providing the necessary data to those who need it.

Far too many business owners carry the title of "President and Treasurer" in fact if not in title. No one has access to the top financial position. Consequently, no one has access to vital information. No one else knows anything. This is the way the boss wants it. The "help" can't do anything or make any decisions until the head man says, "Yes." Yet, no matter how competent the president may be, he cannot do well the tasks of president, chief policy officer, chief operating officer, and chief financial officer all at the same time, forever.

All companies of any size need the services of a strong and competent internal financial executive, not simply a bookkeeper and an accountant who rewrites the figures the bookkeeper gives him, and not "outside financial help" to perform internal functions. When I find someone who is getting his financial statements made up by an outsider, then I know that sooner or later there is going to be a real problem in that company. I also know that this is where I will find the little old maiden lady bookkeeper being kept alive by the outside accountant, because she is his insurance policy. It's somewhat like the little kid who gets paid to catch flies, so he leaves the screen door open.

Some companies, of course, can't afford a professional financial officer on a regular basis. But in far too many family owned companies, the accounting system is on a par with that in the corner barbershop. The boss developed the accounting system himself and he tinkers with it periodically. I don't like a pilot who repairs his own instruments. The type who says, "It's O.K. I always fly south when I mean north because I put the compass in backwards." What bothers me is that he may know how to adjust for certain discrepancies in his system, but it makes me terribly nervous that he's the only one who knows the problem. I really become nervous when he tries to explain the peculiarities of his system to someone else.

HELPING TO FIND OUT WHERE IT HURTS

The older I get, the more orthodox I become. I have a basic suspicion of clever accounting systems that you "sort of" understand. If the owner manager would put more orthodoxy into his accounting system, he would earn more money, pay more taxes, keep more money, and everyone would be better off. Every firm needs competent financial management that will argue with top management, and not sit there and act like a co-conspirator. (Owner managers who don't have that kind of responsible financial management should ask themselves what price they're paying for their secrecy.)

I'm sorry if developing a new accounting system eliminates the job now done by mother, but for the sake of the business and its employees, mother should be asked, please, to find a new activity. She may take up gardening or social work; but she should keep her hands out of the books, because the president can't argue easily with that kind of accounting. There are all kinds of good controller-type accountants available for the management team of a family owned company. By this, I don't mean "ex-auditors" who just want to make sure no one has their hand in the petty cash drawer. I'm not concerned here with that type of accounting control. I'm concerned with the use of accounting data to explain. In my point of view, an accounting system is like a flight plan from destination A to destination B. It requires a known objective, a known path and a reasonably accurate method of telling the pilot where he is at any given stage of the flight.

An accounting system is to be understood. It's not there to impress. If the system is designed by the accountant to confuse, change accountants. That's the easiest way. Non-accountant managers in business find it difficult to understand accounting because its philosophy is almost never well explained to them. Accounting is interesting; it just takes a better than average accountant to explain the system. The business owner needs to find an accountant who wants him to understand.

Many business owners make no effort to institute an orthodox accounting system simply because they do not know what such a system involves. Perhaps someone has told them that "recognized accounting principles" are not an exact science and there are multiple ways for managing the same transaction. They figure that if the "pros" can't make up their mind how to indicate a transaction, then any method will do.

The fact is that in this day of shortages, profit squeezes, inflation, and extensive government regulation, any method will not do. While there are many ways of indicating a specific type of transaction, the accounting method within individual companies is designed to record the transaction in the manner most useful to that company. An experienced accountant can develop a system for an individual company which can take advantage of the variations to the benefit of that company and provide management with the kind of information and options it needs in order to function profitably.

Accounting is the language of business. Just because a business owner is not fluent in the language does not mean that he cannot learn to speak it. A well-versed accountant will help the business owner to learn it. He will explain the components of a good accounting system in terms the business owner can understand, and he will help him to understand the benefits of such a system. Although I am not interested in writing a handbook for establishing accounting systems, I am concerned that the business owner must understand a few of the basic ingredients that he should find in a well-designed system.

One of these records is known as the Balance Sheet, a statement which shows the fundamental soundness of a company by reflecting monthly its financial position at month end through the relationship of its assets to its liabilities. The balance sheet is a standardized form which summarizes the information which a company has been recording in its books and translates those records into readable form. These sheets list what the company did and how it stands.

The Income Statement sometimes also known as the Earnings Report or Statement of Profit and Loss is the monthly report which records the operating activities of a company year. It matches the amount of revenue received from selling goods or services and other income sources against the costs and other outlays to arrive at a net profit or loss for the period. Monthly Income Statements have headed off many near-disasters.

Because of the need for timely recognition by management for corrective action, all companies should additionally develop their records for use in a cost accounting system. Such a system of accounting can charge a proportionate share of all costs—sales administration, plant, etc.—so that the price of each product or service reflects the real cost of producing that product or providing that service, and not just the cost of raw materials and labor in the case of manufacturing or the cost of sales or labor in the case of service. It allows a company a more realistic picture in designing the pricing structure of goods or services.

But perhaps the greatest of all management tools is the "Budget" sometimes called the Pro Forma P & L. Like the budget for a household, the budget for a business is a tool for dealing with the future and making some educated guesses about the reality of that future. It is a tool which enables the businessman to set a goal for the future, take the steps which are necessary to attain that goal and be able to evaluate and correct errors in the process. In its simplest form, the budget is a projected statement of profit and loss. It makes assumptions about the expenditures the businessman expects to make in the next year and the revenue he expects to generate.

In preparing the budget, the businessman is forced to make a prognosis about what he can *plan* to spend and what he can *plan* to receive in the year ahead and in the months and quarters following. The businessman needs a written plan by which he can evaluate his performance. If his goals have been translated into figures, and he has compiled at the end of each period real figures to compare with his projections, he can make a much better job of guessing the next time around. This is called profit planning.

A good accountant will also help the business owner work with an understanding of such concepts as profit centers, ratio analysis, forecasting, and the difference between profit and cash flow. An orthodox accounting system provides a "third party" view necessary to a growing business. Figures can record the operation of the business free from the emotional strain of personal relationships. The need for such a non-personal means of presenting data relationships becomes vital as a company grows.

It takes a different kind of talent to go from the shirt-sleeved founder with four employees who handled every problem himself, as it developed, to the owner manager of a company that has a $5-$10 million annual sales volume and employes 200 people. Looking at performance through the focus of cold-blooded figures rather than through the emotional overtones of individual managers eliminates many of the personality disputes which can develop when many managers become responsible for the profitable growth of the company. As the company grows, it becomes more and more important to deal with facts rather than with personal opinion. Too many owner managers tend to look at their problems from the point of view of either an employee or shareholder and base their opinions on these points of view, rather than viewing problems as a professional manager charged with operating a growing concern at a profit.

ACCOUNTING—THE TEXTBOOK OF A FAMILY OWNED COMPANY

All good ideas must come from knowledge, but the divulgence of knowledge, "information", is not widespread in family owned companies. In many cases the founder president maintains his power by actually withholding information with the aid of his loyal bookkeeper. The boss doesn't say that he deliberately withholds information. What he says is that the help wouldn't understand so he doesn't tell them. So what's the difference?

In a great many companies, the boss could probably show his managers a balance sheet with a "Reserve for Discrepancy" of $10,000 or $100,000 in the middle of it, and they wouldn't catch it, because they don't know how to read the statement. Whose fault is this? What the boss is really saying through his refusal to share information about the company and his unwillingness to teach his employees how to understand his financial data, is that he does not really want anyone else's opinion or judgment. His business is different, and he has made it so. Only he understands it. "The help" does not have the experience to aid him.

When I talk about the secrecy of the boss, and his reluctance to communicate accounting data to "the help," I am not talking about lower level employees. I am referring to the management level employee, the small, but vital, number of men who implement the policies established by the owner. If these men don't know the results of their endeavors and can't see that their contribution to the company results in success, then they are playing in the dark.

I'm not suggesting that the information should be put on the bulletin board or published as a plant-wide release. I am suggesting that if the business owner does not have a key group, an executive committee, a task force of his top two or three or dozen department heads and officers zeroed in on what he's trying to accomplish and how he is going about achieving his goal, then he doesn't have any management leaders in his company. He only has management followers.

Most accounting systems in closed corporations were set up as a device either to cheat the IRS or to keep the employees ignorant, or to keep the partners ignorant, or perhaps to accomplish all three things. They were created as a necessary evil to satisfy government regulations. Historically, founders are known for activity and ability in the field of production or sales, not finance. Few greenshaded accountants start businesses (and those that do are often the worst offenders with respect to making knowledge available to other middle managers.)

Consequently, the role of the accounting system is often to obscure instead of to inform. Financial data is rarely given to the people who need it to make operating judgments. If the role of the controller in a family firm is to hide the data from the operating management, then how can the management team do anything other than play industrial Pin-The-Tail-on-The-Donkey? They pin the tail where they think it should go. Unfortunately, they are blindfolded by secrecy. Instead of shedding any light on the situation, the boss only announces, "You sure are stupid. Why didn't you put your efforts in the right place." In effect, this establishes a double standard for measuring performance, one for the boss, and one for the help.

The concept of a modern accounting system however, is that it is an educational system to assist managers in making better decisions about the resources within their supervision. It is a further method of increasing the managerial ability of the key personnel. The managers should not have to go out of town to participate in this kind of development program. It should be an on-going part of their employment in the company.

If a manager is held accountable for the activities of a given department, he needs some system on which to evaluate his achievement. An accounting system properly designed can provide such an evaluation. It can show him how he is doing in comparison with past years, and it can tell him how well he is doing in the current year in relation to his projections. It can help him examine alternative costs to alternative revenues within his responsibility and give him some means of determining the proper ratio. It can help him decide whether to trim his labor force or take on new projects and additional people. It can help him "make or buy." A good accounting system with proper communication of accumulated data is an invaluable tool for all management in before-the-fact planning and after-the-fact evaluation.

The accounting system should be used as an informational device to aid management in doing its job, not as an evasive system to minimize the owner's tax load. I don't exclude "tax management" as a part of good planning, but I do think that it has been entirely too strongly emphasized. If a business owner is interested in really minimizing his taxes, all he has to do is lose money, do something stupid and close the doors. He'll pay no taxes for the rest of his life.

If the business owner is interested in making money, then he will have to spend his time in areas where he can use his talent to generate a profit. He can't afford to waste it in areas where he is not competent. And he can't afford to waste other people's time and talent by refusing to provide them the basic information upon which their management decisions rest. Instead, he should hire the most competent financial manager he can find.

What the business owner wants and needs is a person who can think in terms of numerical values for the future; someone who can take as much responsibility as the owner can entrust to him. His job is to provide a management information system for the people who are on the organization chart. There can't be such a thing as too keen a financial insight in the use of the company's money. The duty of such a financial manager is definitely not limited to balancing the books. He's going to institute a budgetary and cost allocation accounting system; he's going to help draw up some long range financing plans, market projections, monthly balance sheets, and income statements. He may even have some suggestions for better management controls, computer-based forecasting, and a host of other management aids.

If the business owner does not know whether he has a good financial man in that slot in his company, then he should ask questions of him and his peers. People with talent like to show that they have this talent. It's never been impertinent to ask a pretty girl to enter a beauty contest. It is not impertinent to ask a financial man to be judged by others in his field or in related fields.

Each owner manager's accounting system will differ because it must be tailored to fit the individual company. It is not difficult to make the accounting system informative and useful. The fact that the owner manager, himself, does not know how to do it should not deter him from having it done. Any banker or outside financial advisor will be glad to help him find the right people to set up the system and make it operative. That advice is worth seeking before it is too late.

Chapter Seven

Gaining Commitment
from Outside Advisors

ADVISORS ARE NOT FOREVER

There can be no long-term success for the owner managed business if the founder is going to maintain a sentimental philanthropic association with second class advisors. Among the advisors he normally chooses are lawyers, bankers, accountants, insurance men, and consultants of various kinds. In the early days of owning his own business, when being business owner meant getting dirty at honest labor and staying out of debt, the quality of advice available to him was probably a reflection of his bank account, minimal. Now, thirty years later, his million dollar business is probably still dependent upon second-story legal talent and banking connections.

The owner manager should realize that he is under no compulsion to maintain his advisors forever. Professional fees take into account terminations by clients. Advisors should serve only on the condition of a continuing usefulness and commitment. Too many owner managers do first-class work and provide first-class service themselves, but then insist on surrounding themselves with second-class advisors while not paying them second-class fees.

I take a dim view of the quality of the advisors to most business owners. They're not real advisors. They are economic piranhas preying upon tired and unimaginative owner managers. Their credentials are tenure and the ease with which the owner can do business with them. They patch up their own mistakes as well as his, drag their feet on his time, resist change, and too often transfer their insecurity to their clients. With the assistance of good tailors, good barbers, and ready conversation, such advisors can cloak characteristics of selfishness, non-commitment, insensitivity, incompetence and obsolescence under the guise of success. Too often they take the job of advisor not for the challenge and commitment but for the money, prestige, influence, or "inside" knowledge that it is able to create.

Such men have no idea of the purpose or the needs of the company other than for their own financial gain. It is too often a private vehicle for their own aims and needs. Because they have never taken the time to truly understand the business owner's goals, their role as advisor is not to assist him as the president. The purpose of their advice is for his payment, and they return what minimal service is necessary to maintain it. They are another kind of economic hat check girl.

To accept this kind of advisor is for the business owner to accept second-class citizenship, a continuous feeling of insecurity, that he is doing something wrong, that he somehow does not deserve the success he has earned, that if he changes anything or anyone, what he has earned will all be taken away from him. He's paying intellectual blackmail and doesn't know it.

COMPETENCE IS THE CRITERION FOR CHOOSING ADVISORS

All of the professional advisors to the closed corporation must be examined periodically and their tenure should be neither assumed nor assured. They need to be periodically reviewed regarding their continued relevancy and contribution to the solutions of the problems at hand or in the offing. They must be retained for their positive and creative contribution rather than for their penchant for maintaining the status quo with which they are comfortable and for which they can get paid to keep the business out of "trouble." It is like a fellow I once met who said his job was to keep elephants away from the saloon. When asked, "Gosh you don't do much?" He would always reply, "You don't see any elephants around here, do you?" That kind of advisor you don't need. Other elephant chasers you don't need:

The lawyer who was fine in the pick and shovel days but lacks the legal sophistication necessary to deal with new corporate problems, the requirements of estate planning, and the increasing influence of government regulation, and taxation on your growing operations. If you're his biggest client, be careful. Where else do you suppose he's learning?

The outside accountant simply audits or posts the figures he gets from the little old lady with the moustache, or just adjusts them for acceptance by the IRS. The advice you get here is minimal. This is hardly the way for you to analyze the transactions of a million dollar business. Remember, it's your money he's playing with.

What confidence do you have in consultants without honor in their own town or current competency in their own field in the judgment of their peers and their ex-clients?

How much faith can you have in the advice of insurance men whose client list mainly consists of old school pals, fellow club members, nostalgic sports fans, or companies you never heard of?

How much assistance in long range planning do you get from bankers serving out their preretirement or fearing for their own financial security? What special insight do you suppose this provides them for your future?

The list is endless. Yet, the president of a family owned business *must* let outside advisors help him do his job because he has neither the time nor the expertise to do it alone anymore. If he were honest with himself, he would have to admit that his own talents are limited, fully committed, to be sure, but inadequate in too many areas. Rather than search for famous out-of-town specialists for a one time "catch-up" session, he must discover that his best advisors are found close to home. Because their thinking has become ghettoized, too many business owners feel that the best advisors are out-of-town, and whisk off to association meetings in New York or San Francisco to patch up in two days a mess it's taken them twenty years to create. Yet, to do them any good, they must seek their own experts at home. The best lawyer, the best banker, the best accountant for the business owner must be back home, not someplace else.

The business owner must look outside of the parochial circle, however, in which he lives. There are good bankers near him that he's not doing business with, because he thinks they don't understand. There are great estate planners but he doesn't do business with them, either, for the same reason. There are great accountants, good consultants, and fine law firms all around, but the boss does business with "Whosis and Whatsis" three flights up, because it's "comfortable" and he thinks it's going to be cheaper. It isn't in the end. It's like trying to save money on the vermouth instead of on the gin.

The business owner should list his advisors on a sheet of paper. This is his world. He may find that he has filled it with people who can't or won't help him and it is then that he goes out of town to compensate for their inadequacies. It's just like a guy who can't find love at home; he goes outside, and you know what we think of him.

BANKERS AREN'T BUM BUSINESSMEN

If he doesn't respect and work with a good banker in his own bank, he doesn't have to find some financial genius out of town; he just has to change banks. It's like kissing a girl with his eyes open. If he doesn't like what he sees, he shouldn't close his eyes; he should change girls. Bankers should be chosen for their competence and progressiveness. Bankers must be the worthy recipient of the owner's trust. They must evidence concern with and commitment to the business owner's future planning, both corporate and personal.

The business owner should consider how much time he spends with his banker. How good is his banker? Does he really confide in him? Does he give him maybe a couple of hours a month? Does he keep him informed, good months and bad months? Does he sit down and talk to his banker about what he thinks is important and let the banker look at the numbers, or does he feel that if he did that, the bank would call in his note?

When I was younger, I used to think that bankers were backward because they wouldn't lend me any money when I needed it. How come when they had all the money, they were so stupid and I was so bright? But in recent years, I've met a lot of great bankers and I've got infinite respect for their judgment. They want to talk to business owners. Bankers feel they could help, if they were asked. They'd like to be honest with the boss, but he lies to them. They're not going to be impolite and lose his account; they just won't help.

I've made it a rule that I won't buy my own ideas if I can't sell them to a banker. It is possible that any single banker might not accept my idea because I didn't explain it to him clearly. But if I can't explain myself to two or three bankers and have them accept my idea, then I will not buy it myself. The best piece of advice I got came some years ago from a little old immigrant tailor. He told me, "Son, don't never buy what you can't sell, and that includes your opinion."

LAWYERS ARE MORE THAN FIXERS

Too many business owners think talking to their lawyer is something like talking to God. There are good lawyers and bad lawyers. The business owner must find one with whom he's willing to be honest and stop using them as co-conspirators and undercover men.

A lawyer's chief function is not to bail out the boss when the company truck hits the school bus. He's not there just to limit the company's liability, collect from deadbeats, intimidate the union, act as novelist for the board meeting, and referee in family fights. He's not really being used fully in these situations. A lawyer is a trained professional who has known the inside of a hundred family businesses, but the boss hesitates to let him understand his company and his operation.

Attorneys are needed who understand the implications of new Governmental regulations on the socio-economic environment in which the company operates. A lawyer should be consulted about plans for succession and the mangement transfer of the president's ownership interests. If he doesn't understand, all the business owner has to do is to find one who does. The whole field of estate planning is one in which an attorney should become involved. The problems of long term commitment to serve the betterment of employees in pension trusts and profit-sharing is a matter for an attorney. In short, planning for the future is as much his concern, or it should be as his occasional stints at bailing the business owner out of trouble. The business owner should confer with his lawyer about the creation of a working outside board. If he says, "forget it, you don't need such a board," I suggest the owner change attorneys.

In today's complex world, the entrepreneurial attorney with his office over the barbershop is probably becoming less and less helpful. The emergence in recent years of the medical clinic has been rivalled by the growing importance of the legal clinic, the group practice of lawyers. Bands of legal specialists group themselves together into law firms where each attorney is an outstanding specialist who practices in his own field, and the firm can accumulate detailed information on the family owned business from all the attorneys who work directly with the owner. The president, therefore, doesn't have to transfer data from man to man every time his problems enlarge, and he needs the assistance of a new kind of specialist. Many heads do help when there are many problems.

ACCOUNTANTS ARE NOT JUST TAX SHELTERERS

Business owners consider their accountant primarily as their personal gladiator with the IRS. That's a shame. I don't really consider that man's purpose on earth is to spend his life as a tax avoider. Maybe I'm naive, but I think we should spend the bulk of our business efforts trying to earn a profit, not hide it.

An accountant, like a lawyer or a banker or any competent advisor, if he's any good, is a widely acquainted man with clients in many business fields both similar and different in nature and product. The business owner should be doing business with the best firm in town. He should be long past the individual practitioner who in turn depends upon the little old bookkeeper.

The family owned company really needs a 35 year old narrow-lapelled, white shirt, buttoned-down CPA who works for a first class firm. The owner should not be fooled into thinking the accountant is stupid just because he's only making a third the money the owner is, and that he doesn't understand the business. He's not supposed to take the owner's risks or rewards. His strong suit is fiscal discipline.

The number of business owners who use competent public accounting firms is miniscule. They have no idea what good, sound, competent fiscal discipline can do. Instead they do business with a second-rater who can't help them because they're comfortable with second raters. Because second raters can give the owner the same answers they gave him five years ago, ten years ago, they are not threatening. Also they throw in preparation of his mother-in-law's 1040 as a "favor"—(no charge, the boss thinks. He's wrong. He just can't find it). He thinks that adding up the columns and showing a bigger number in the southeast corner than was there last time is all there is to it. Well, it isn't.

Accounting is not a tax avoidance system. Accounting today is a managerial tool to distribute information to people who take collective action to generate a profit. It's an analysis. It's an educational system dependent upon its books, its library and its flow of information. A competetent outside accountant will substantiate this, and explain it in ways that a second-rate, secretive bookkeeper never can. He'll explain what he means with budgets, monthly financial statements, cost accounting systems and many other financial controls. He will help to make data available and useful to management at all levels. His assistance is invaluable in making long term financial decisions which can effect the ultimate destiny of the business.

Furthermore, a competent auditor may inform the business owner, "Look, I can't put up with your bookkeeper. Let's get a decent financial manager in here, because I'm not going to compensate for the inadequacies of your internal financial system." That's good advice. And Gertrude will fight it all the way. A second-rate accountant has been her job security for years. Their collusion has kept both of them employed.

INSURANCE AGENTS AREN'T ALL POLICY PUSHERS

Just because insurance agents are generally friendly, articulate, persuasive, and value their time like any other top notch professional, it's no reason to assume that they are glib, immoral, fast talking, hustlers of dubious services who should be avoided at all costs. The leading insurance men in any community are among the most respected men in town because of their commitment to the needs of the people in their community. Surely, the product of any one insurance carrier is competitive with that of many others; but it is far more important to do business with a man whom the owner can trust than with the best "deal." If they are honest, most owner managers are not too sure they always understand thoroughly the insurance they are buying; therefore confidence in the agent is essential.

It is essential that the agent get to know the company. It is important that he get to know the owner and understand his requirements and limitations. The business owner needs his insurance agent's judgment, his evaluation, and his explanation of the various financial and other alternatives available. If the casualty agent is a C.P.C.U. (Chartered Property and Casualty Underwriter) and the life insurance underwriter is a C.L.U. (Chartered Life Underwriter), an owner manager has a better chance of getting competent insurance advice.

If the business owner thinks that he can become expert in the insurance field just because he is expert in his own field, he is deluding himself. Insurance has become a most sophisticated field, overlapping in many areas of involvement with the law, taxation, investment and banking. In addition, the insurance field helps to fulfill the ever growing needs by the business owner for casualty coverages of all descriptions.

The relatively recent concept of "estate planning" is a new and vital business ingredient in the business owner's future and it is generally misunderstood. Until recently, its thrust was of interest only to the very wealthy. Most of the rest of humanity had a more urgent problem, that of assuring themselves that they would eat regularly. Insurance meant covering burial costs and repaying automobile repairs. Over the past 30 years, as businessmen discoverd increasing needs for help in leaving anything of consequence to their chosen beneficiaries, specialists in business insurance have concentrated on the business owner market as a fertile field for the use of insurance coverage for many funding purposes; buy and sell agreements, trust opportunities, stock option and transfer plans, and fringe benefit programs of all descriptions. Invariably, success in solving the needs of other businessmen has made many insurance men wealthy.

CONSULTANTS AREN'T EVIDENCES OF WEAKNESS

Many businesses find that they develop problems which are not within the specific province of lawyers, bankers, accountants or insurance men. The problems need solving, but often neither these advisors nor the owner managers have the time nor the expertise to find a solution. Perhaps they are so engrossed in specific aspects of the business that they cannot see the forest for the trees. Perhaps, it is their own performance which is at fault and which the owner manager is afraid or unable to evaluate. Often, specific personnel or technical problems demand answers which are not available from other members of the management team.

Difficulties of this nature are the province of a whole range of specialists known as consultants. These men are experts in handling specific types of problems within a business; ineffective production operations, personnel conflicts, management and material procurement, fringe benefit programs, marketing re-organization, successor evaluation and education and long range planning. Unlike other advisors, top consultants are not usually employed on a long-term basis. Their function is to minister to specific problems and then get out. This does not mean that they may not be called back at another time to deal with another problem, but their relationship with the firm is usually on a short-term basis to advise on a specific situation or series of situations.

The average business owner greets the suggestion that he needs a consultant with the same relish that he would if someone told him he needed a psycho-analyst, but the consultant is not in the couch business. He doesn't expect the business owner to replay his childhood. He's not interested in the twists of his libido. He will want to take a long look at the business and its needs, its markets, its products; its assets; how the owner works with his managers, advisors, and directors; how he develops his employees; how the management and employee groups work together and the results of the owner's management style. He may have some pretty strong suggestions about the things which must be changed in order to avoid a strike, head off a take-over, develop/acquire new products/markets, establish pension funds, increase market share, recruit top-level management, or counter a host of other problems. Many businesses are strong and thriving today because of the providential probing of an experienced and competent consultant.

To the owner who says, "I can't afford a top consultant," I offer the reminder; there is nothing more costly than bad advice or no advice at all, when the walls come tumbling down.

HOW TO USE ADVICE

Finally, even though he may have gotten the best available advisors, the business owner may not be getting the real benefit of their talent. He rarely spends time with them together rubbing elbows over problems around the same table. Instead, the average business owner functions like a king on a throne. He summons Advisor A to talk with him. He listens. He argues and discards. Then, in turn, he summons Advisors B, C, D, E, and F and auditions them individually to test their answers. He functions this way in order to "confirm" his opinion. The rest of their advice he neither hears nor takes. (See Figure 10). He's really practicing self-taught brain surgery.

What a waste of time and effort to go through this rigamarole of selective non-disclosure. If he really wants his advisors to help him, the business owner will have to abandon this watercooler schedule. Instead of ladling out bits of knowledge to each person in individual sessions, he should invite them all to share the problem. He must let each advisor gather a little side support from his peers.

"THE ADVISORS"
or LET EVERY RASPUTIN HAVE HIS TURN — BUT THEY'LL NEVER MEET ᴛᴏ AGREE !

Figure 10.

He must let each one know what the others know, so that together they can surround a problem and help him find the answer. He'll be amazed by the results. What he will have each time he arranges such a session is a private business seminar of his own. (See Figure 11). The instructors are competent informed professionals whose major concern is to assist the business owner in maximizing his options by offering viable alternatives to his plans and needs. Those men can assist him and his board in a periodic audit of his actions by providing data on which corporate implementation can be based, continued or terminated and by introducing into his thinking other opinions than his own.

When he does bring them together periodically, they'll tell him that he is going to have to do things differently. He's going to have to institute a budgetary and cost allocation accounting system. He'll need some long range financing plans, more market projections, some employee training, some organization building, capital equipment planning, etc., etc. What a list! That's why nobody starts a business with professional advisors and accounting systems and budgetary controls and organizational charts. If an owner had all that stuff, he wouldn't have had the time to make, buy, or sell his products and services and make money. So first things came first.

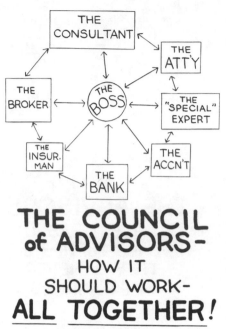

THE COUNCIL
of ADVISORS-
HOW IT
SHOULD WORK-
ALL TOGETHER!

Figure 11.

The vital role which a competent council of advisors plays in the functioning of an owner-managed business was made remarkably clear to me recently. A contractor I know who operates a 25 million dollar business employing about 250 people was faced with a deep financial crisis as the result of a combination of several bad job cost over-runs and some major estimating errors due to faulty information. He called me one day in panic. He was in bad trouble.

I had known this man for about a year. When we first met, he was very cagey. He probably would not have told me the time of day without asking why I wanted to know—or what I was going to do with the answer when I got it. Gradually we began to build up some trust between us. However, early in our association, I examined his advisors. His lawyer, who was close to eighty, had originally incorporated the firm 43 years before for his father. He was certainly not a very impressive attorney for a prominent construction company. His accountant who handled his finances did the company books on the side; his major source of revenue came at income tax time as the financial mouthpiece of the medical community in the town in which the firm was located. Although this owner manager virtually owned one of the largest companies in town, and maintained large deposits in two leading banks, he had never really levelled with the president of either bank, because he was afraid of both gossip at the club and unsolicited advice on his management practices.

One of the first changes suggested was the development of a council of advisors. We found a top notch young corporate attorney from the major law firm in a nearby city. We sent the individual tax practitioner on his way and brought in a major accounting firm to redo the entire accounting system. We scheduled several lengthy meetings with one of the bankers and laid out plans for the future capital needs of the business. We had to locate a management consultant with extensive personnel experience to monitor the company management recruitment programs. We had an insurance man who was a C.P.C.U. recheck the company's liability insurance and drew up suggestions for revising the total corporate insurance program. For nearly a year all these men met quarterly with the owner and his financial vice president as a council of advisors to them.

When the call came through that day, I was concerned, but not alarmed. I knew this business owner had the resources to deal with his problems. I suggested he call a special meeting of all of his advisors and his key managers as early as it could be scheduled.

As the situation was outlined by the president, the advisors moved quickly. Fully aware of the company's plans and resources from previous council meetings, they acted like a real pro team. The accounting firm helped the firm's Vice President and his staff prepare a detailed cost analysis of the overruns for use by the attorneys in seeking a price increase from the developer. The personnel consultant made recommendations as to management shifts that could be made in both the field and the office to put together a "top team" to try to roll back some of the impending job costs forecasted. The attorney and the insurance counselor were able to seek redress against the engineering firm that had provided much of the faulty data on which the estimates were made in good faith.

For its part, the bank agreed to make available a line of credit for substantial amounts of money secured against the general credit of the firm which they knew to be sound despite the imminent liquidity crunch occasioned by the untimely sequence of events. While there was no way to negate the effects of the unfortunate management errors made by the company, near catastrophe was averted; collective, remedial and self reinforcing actions were taken promptly, and there was no panic to add to the business owner's troubles. He was satisfied that he was not "alone." After the dust settled, he called me again. "Can you imagine what a mess I'd be in now, if I hadn't created that advisors council?" he asked. I certainly could imagine it, and I told him so. "Well," he growled. "I just wanted to say thanks. I used to worry about telling my advisors so much about my company. But, I sure am glad, now, that I did."

Hopefully, it will not require a crisis before business owners appreciate the value of top quality advisors acting in concert. The peace of mind that comes from knowing that they are supported by the best minds in a variety of professional fields should have value enough to convince business owners that they can't afford either cheap or conflicting advice. All growing companies need the services of the finest advisors they can find acting together in continued commitment to help the business owner and his management plan and act with confidence on the more difficult decisions resulting from success.

Chapter Eight

Creating a Working Board

A SUCCESSFUL PRESIDENT NEEDS REVIEW

No well run corporation, family owned or not, can operate efficiently without a periodic review of its chief executive officer. Yet, his employees, his managers, and his advisors cannot provide this review. They are the paid help. The business owner can get their opinion anytime, and, often, he can get any opinion he wishes. So where does the owner manager go for candid review, inspiration and support when the going gets tough? This is the job for an outside board of directors.

Unfortunately, most family-owned companies do not have real boards of directors. They have a group of melon splitters or co-conspirators—mother and dad's old cronies, sons, a few management employees who rubber stamp the decisions the boss makes or relatives employed one way or another by the company. This activity is useless. If the business owner wants to get together with his management, he should hold a staff meeting; if he wants opinions from friends or relatives, he should invite them over for dinner, hold a bridge party or rent the club for an evening, but, those events are not board meetings.

The founder of a family-owned business is the architect of his company. In truth, his company might best be described not as a family corporation, not a closely-held corporation, but rather a custom-built corporation. His challenge is how to adapt it to the next generation of managers who, in turn, will permit it to remain a valuable thing in a changing world. Reared in the rough and tumble atmosphere of the plant or the truck, he has not entirely dismissed attitudes learned with the boys, even though he now spends most of his time in the office.

At some point, either out of desperation or loneliness, the owner president becomes tired breathing the empty air of his executive suite. No longer considered one of the boys on the floor, and too proud to move his office permanently to the club or the golf course, the founder president has no choice but to face up to the problems inherent in planning for the succeful continuity of his business, if he wishes the company to continue. To do that well, he needs the assistance of men whom he can trust, and men who believe in him and in his goals. Privately-held companies die much faster and more violently than large, publicly held companies. The smaller structure of the family corporation cannot withstand or absorb errors in judgment with the serenity of the public companies. A good board of outside directors can help head off critical mistakes. It can provide a system of checks and balances that becomes so necessary with the increased size and complexity of a growing business. It can require the boss to think things through before acting or insist on action if he's dragging his feet.

One thing is certain. The owner manager cannot go it alone. During his 20 to 30 year tenure in office, the world has changed. Chances are his single-minded persistence in building his business has seriously hampered his ability to change with it. Therefore, although he has built his company from scratch, the owner president is usually not too sure how to become an effective professional manager in his family corporation. He is usually exceptionally capable only in a narrow band of activity. He has a specific talent as engineer, technician, salesman, designer or operator which enabled him to found and develop his business. He has been so busy building his company that he has not had the opportunity to look objectively into any other business. He lives and thinks or dreams alone. He has become a corporate celibate. His board structure, which relies heavily on rubber stampers for members, is by default really designed by him to continue this situation.

THE BOARD AS IT OFTEN IS

Unfortunately, the average American director is unqualified to hold his position. It is a matter of arithmetic. There are a million corporations in the United States. If each corporation had only 3 directors, that would make a total of 3 million directors in the country. Serving the 20-30 thousand publicly owned companies in this country there are perhaps no more than 100 to 200 thousand real directors. The remainder of the 3 million are directors in the privately owned companies, mostly legal puppets without purpose, training, qualification, or responsibility. At best they supply silence and/or acquiescence to the all powerful owner president. For his part the president considers them a nuisance. Just a cheap (no fee, just dinner) way to "reward" (lots of prestige) faithful (unquestioning) old, grateful, dependent relatives or employees (out of date) or else a legal requirement necessitated by the chief executive's option to be treated as a corporation rather than as a proprietorship, which is the way he thinks. In this case he puts on "his" Board the co-conspirators who help him get the best of all worlds: attorneys for limitation on his liability, accountants for preferential tax treatment, or bankers for access to capital without surrender of equity.

Among these 3 million directors in the United States the most common occupation is "mother." Now, please understand, I love my mother—but I can't see what contribution mother makes as a member of the Board. Then, if besides mother there is also added Aunt Louise, Dad's old partner, and a retired dentist—what the owner ends up with is a Board of "yes-men"—a rubber stamp group controlled by the owner-president. These directors usually offer no constructive criticism, don't have much to say, if anything, and generally just approve whatever the "boss" wants them to approve. The boss says, "Charlie, sign here." Charlie says, "What for?" and the boss says, "Never mind, just sign." . . . and Charlie signs. In many cases, the required formal Board Meetings are not very formal at all, and the company attorney oversees the writing of the minutes just to make sure everything is properly and legally recorded, if the meeting was even held at all. Otherwise intelligent owner-managers permit this situation to exist in order to maintain their unreviewed control over the company. By stacking the Board with relatives and employees, the owner maintains absolute control over the board of directors because the shareholders, the officers, and the directors are all the same people and they all owe their allegiance to the boss. Such corporate inbreeding is hardly conducive to innovation, growth, or perpetuation. Multiple subsidiary corporations for dependent operations, realty investment, and other tax minimizing schemes all have the same characteristics. The watchword is "outsiders stay out."

Although this kind of board provides the owner manager the type of control he seeks, occasionally it puts him in an uncomfortable position. If any of his decisions or attitudes are questioned, the president takes on the role of the "accused." For a second-generation president, the inheritor, the circumstances created by such a board can become intolerable. He must often try to operate in an environment where greedy relatives are so divided and antagonistic regarding proper goals of the corporation and the position of "their company" to provide for them that bitter stalemates or family fights are inevitable.

ELIMINATE THE TOKEN BOARD

To avoid perpetuating such an environment, a conscientious president needs a competent working board of outside directors to serve as sounding board, challenger, monitor and enforcer. The board can then be a yardstick by which the chief executive can measure himself in a professional association where he can exchange views with his peers. It can give him moral support and an opportunity for discussion.

The president needs someone to help him perform, men with whom he can be frank. This is a prime requirement. He needs people whom he can respect and who respect him. The board can make him perform by virtue of its power of review and its power of veto.

Some presidents, of course, maintain that they receive sufficient stimulation from their sporadic forays with customers, suppliers, advisors and employees. The need-fulfillment of an active board of directors is like a good marriage. Marriage is not a necessary institution. There are mistresses; but mistresses do not help in building anything together.

A formally organized board divorced from the internal organization of the family is not formed overnight. Its consideration could begin either when annual sales volume approaches $1 million, when multiple levels of management become necessary to run the company, or when Dad realizes he wants to perpetuate his dream. At this point the company begins to merit formal concern over its continuity and long term direction as opposed to the pressure and priority of the day-to-day management actions necessary in its earlier days.

The board of directors in a privately held company should not, however, be confused with the board of a publicly owned company. While many of their duties and responsibilities will be similar, the focus of these responsibilities is different. The primary function of a board of directors in a publicly held corporation is to represent the interests of the shareholders in profitability, successful management, and growth. The primary function of the board of directors in a privately held firm must be to provide for the continuity of the business.

OTHERS WANT TO HELP

I have been fascinated to watch the changes that take place in some of the companies whose presidents attend our seminars. One of the major areas which these men come prepared to ignore and go back eager to change is the composition of their board of directors. In some cases all the prodding a man really needs is the assurance that he has the right to take his relatives off the board and put other businessmen on it.

A case in point is that of the owner of a chain of office supply stores in the Midwest. At the time we first met he had been in business for about 25 years and was just turning sixty. He figured he had another ten to fifteen years in the business. His only son, 35 years old, attended the seminar with him, and everytime Dad talked about staying around another ten or fifteen years, both the son and the other participants winced visibly. It became evident that this bright young man, himself, might die before he had a chance to assume leadership in his company.

After one of the sessions the son sat down with me and really poured out his concerns. What could he do to solve this problem? He respected his Dad, but the old man really was getting tired of the day-to-day hassle and becoming neglectful of necessary actions. If he would just retire, the son was most willing to assume the burdens of overall management and its responsibilities. He felt sure that his father had many other major areas of interest to which he could devote his time. We talked about the subject of the day which had been a session about developing an outside board of directors. The son began to see that if the company had a working board rather than a collection of family and hangers-on, perhaps there would be some mechanism for solving the problem of succession without destroying Dad.

About four years after the seminar I ran into this young man at a convention. "Congratulate me," he said. "I've just been elected president." I asked him how he managed the change. "I didn't," he replied, "The Board of Directors did it."

He then told me that on the way home from the seminar his father had confided in him that the company really needed some ongoing outside help. The nature of the company had changed considerably from the early days of the business, and the older man felt that the company was missing out on some opportunities, because he didn't know how to develop them. He suggested that the son might want to help him recruit some valuable outside directors for the business. To the young man it was like the opening of a door. He sat down with his father and went over a list of participants from the seminar. They found several likely candidates who lived within an hour of the city in which the company operated. Dad sat on the boards of several civic and charitable organizations and a bank, and he began to look at his fellow directors with new interest. Could those who were not in competitive enterprises but who showed an understanding of the kinds of problems in which the father felt need for help become candidates for the board? For his part, the son, who had completed an M.B.A. at a nearby university 10 years before, reviewed the progress of some fellow graduates and discussed his plans with some of his old instructors. He was particularly impressed by suggestions made by two alumni and an instructor, and he suggested them for consideration to augment Dad's choice of peers.

After they had accumulated a considerable list, father and son sat down together and sifted through it to compile a final list of candidates which varied in backgrounds, business experience, age, special talents, and prior board experience. Those were their first choice. Other names were kept on a back-up list in order of preference, both to serve as additional choices in case of refusal and to provide a reservoir for future changes on the board. Together, father and son approached each candidate and discussed their business with him and asked for his commitment to board duty. To their surprise all accepted. Their company had built such an enviable reputation over the years that those whom they had asked considered the invitation a compliment and a challenge.

For the first few meetings the board dealt largely with other crucial changes in the business: new accounting systems; evaluating and replacing an incompetent manager; modernizing and formalizing budgets for both operational and capital needs; employee benefit programs in order to retain competent help and a market plan for future growth. Early in the second year of its tenure, the board began inquiring about the president's plan for retirement. "It was kind of a bloody session," the son said. "I thought maybe Dad would dissolve the board right then and there." But the old man listened to his peers who explained to him the need for new blood in the organization and the dangers they began to see developing because he would be hanging on too long. It took two more meetings before the founder agreed to a retirement plan. When he finally agreed, it was like giving the founder a new lease on life.

Instead of fretting about the operational aspects of the business, he began planning for its future and the presidential changeover. He delegated many of the tasks that had been his alone to others down the line. He and his son spent busy hours constructing a future plan for a business they could both cherish. When the agreed-on retirement date came, the founder took the advice of one of his board members and he and his wife left on a six month's cruise so that the son could assume his new duties without Dad peering over his shoulder.

I've kept in touch with this company from time to time. The son, as the new president, has much of the same vigor as his father. He has expanded the business into several nearby states, and is even planning on acquiring a subsidiary office interior planning firm. His father has found that he is sought after by numerous organizations which wish to use his business experience and his available time. For this particular father and son, the development of a competent board with the power to review the president has resulted in a smooth shift of the business from one generation to another.

The experience of this father and son need not be unusual. The founder of any family owned business can dissolve his token board and establish a committed, working board of competent outside directors. The task is not that difficult, once the business owner has become committed to it. Perhaps one of the reasons that the owners of family businesses do not make these moves is that they really do not know how to go about forming such a board of directors; who should serve on it; what their functions should be, and what the owner can expect from their participation.

SOME QUESTIONS ABOUT BOARDS

1. *Who Should Serve on The Board of Directors?* The people who understand best the operation of a family business are other risk taking businessmen. This is not just a plea to remove Dad's sister from the board. It is a recommendation that the makeup of the board be balanced. The business owner should balance off the internal self-interests; family, retainers and employees, with outsiders, other businessmen who are engaged in enterprises different

from his own, who both appreciate and understand the risks he shoulders, whose judgment he respects, and who respect him.

In looking for potential board members, the business owner would do well to omit relatives. Significant problems can occur when family squabbles circumvent the purpose of the board meeting. Very few relatives have much to contribute. The addition of wives and mothers too often invites intrigue and risks misunderstandings. Advice from these quarters is available for the asking at a family dinner party.

If the business owner already has a whole group of uncles and aunts on the board, he is going to have to get rid of them. There is no purpose in having a professionally oriented board of directors stymied by Uncle Willie who thinks that if gold still backed the dollar, the company could have made some money. People who remind one how good the Good Old Days were are useless. Board members need to be people who are going to be involved in the days to come.

Those who get on the board solely through marriage or investment tend to inhibit others who have something to say. Board members who are knowledgeable end up talking down to those who do not understand, and addressing their remarks to the one person in need of lengthy explanations, and the meeting degenerates until it is of no constructive value to anyone. If this type of activity continues for a long period of time, even the most conscientious director ends up feeling that he's involved in a family episode of corporate "show-'n-tell," loses interest, and his contribution diminishes.

The purpose of a board meeting is not to inform Mother but to set policy and otherwise challenge the manager to reach heights he might not reach alone and without allies. If your wife really wants to know what's going on in the business, then invite the directors and advisors over to the house for dinner for the sole purpose of explaining matters to her and answering her questions. They'll understand why they're there; they might even welcome the opportunity.

Subordinates on the board also tend to inhibit the criticism by outsiders and to create rubber stampers whose major contribution on the board is to "yes" the boss. If the board needs their specific technical talents, they may be invited to report *to* the board.

Board membership for those professional advisors such as the lawyers, accountants, consultants and insurance men who are retained by the company raises a definite question of conflict of interest. Who is judging whom? While the varied experience of professionals can provide additional functional tools to management, these specialists are available for their hire and could also be invited to report to the board on specific issues, or for review of their recommendations.

For the most part, retired businessmen are not too effective as board members. Unfortunately, retirement puts too many men out of touch with the contemporary world. It denies them an opportunity for continued stimulation and creative problem-solving. It makes men look back to the days of old glories instead of forward to new challenges. Board members should be active in business. Somehow there comes a point after a man retires that he needs to prove he's busy. No business owner needs to be a social worker and put people on his board so they can avoid cutting the grass on the bias or going shopping with their wife. It is not just a matter of age. People can be underemployed and/or retired at the age of 40, and/or be active at the age of 70. The criterion is that they be active and hold a job that is meaningful. Someone who sits and tolerates the president in order to be "active" is not a fully helpful board member. A director should challenge and add to the owner manager's current understanding of the business and its needs, as well as furnish experience and judgment from their past activities. A talented outsider who has just been retired may have a few years of active contribution but beware of maintaining his tenure on the board.

There should be a balance in the ages of the directors. If all of the directors are contemporaries of the boss, their judgments not only have the overtones of similar experience, but their tenure will coincide with his. Board members should be selected to serve both the founder and the successor. They can bring some measure of past perspective into present planning for the future. Just as family, friends, advisors, or employees do not make good board members, neither do investors. Their opinion on something can be ascertained at a shareholder's meeting.

Who, then, should the business owner consider as prospective board members? He should choose *outsiders to the owner and to his business whose views he cannot acquire or buy for any purpose or at any price.* They should be people who are willing to help him understand his business better by asking penetrating questions. Qualities important in those he chooses as directors are unquestioned integrity, good judgment, problem-solving ability and a personal feeling for action and risk management. As business problems of the modern company increasingly take on political, social, and economic overtones, directors should have in addition to proven past business performance, an awareness, a varied perspective, and an adaptability to understand the changing circumstances of our contemporary world. The kind of management decisions which a board must assist the president to make require more than expertise in a single field, industry, or profession.

2. *Where Does The Owner Find Good Directors?* Men with these qualifications are not discovered easily. Good directors are like good wives: they must be found where a man lives. He just has to become sensitive to the fact that they exist. Most people feel reluctant to get close to people, on a business basis, whom they have met in some other field of endeavor. Mostly the only people they know are already involved in their business in some way. They're either customers, suppliers, advisors, friends, investors, or old buddies in the trade association, and they are rarely objective about either the company or its management.

Directors are peers. They are not part of a superior-subordinate relationship in various pecking orders. Men exist everywhere who are sympathetic to the goals of others. One has only to ask them, and be willing to share his hopes with them, show them where the problems are, where he wants to go, what his strengths are, and what his short suit is, and what he has to work with.

That's the rub. Most people won't be that open with anyone. They are economic atheists. They believe only in themselves; no one can help them, and they suffer alone. The average family corporation president would have a difficult time trying to name three outsiders with whom he would be willing to be completely frank; but if he is not going to be honest, why should he go through the travesty of a board?

He must look around instead of copping out with the tired refrain: "My business is different. Outsiders don't understand my problems." They don't understand his problems, all right, because he calls their facts—opinion—while he calls his opinions—facts. That's the problem. The president has become his own worst enemy. He has permitted the income that has been generated by his company in his lifetime to fool him into thinking that he always knows what he is doing, and that no one else does or ever did. He doesn't know what he is doing or who else could do it as well or better. He never competed for the job.

In truth, potential board members are everywhere. They can be found among the people with whom one associates. This is why it becomes necessary for the president of the closely held company to keep enlarging his circle of acquaintances rather than to depend upon the same group of people who have influenced him in the past. It is kind of an economic substitute for the drive that keeps us looking for the right girl to marry.

Board members are not found by accident. They must be actively sought. The outside director with the potential to put his finger on mistakes in judgment should not be sought just for his technical help but for his perception, perspective and insight.

A board member is there for his opinions, in all areas of his competence, even if it does sometimes mean telling the boss what he doesn't want to hear. Accepting sound advice does not make the boss a second-class puppet. A board member's job is to see that this vehicle called "the business" is continued into the future. He is there to see that the boss develops a successful continuing management and to prevent him from slipping subconsciously into doing what he knows he shouldn't do. A good director is an absolutely secure, competent man. When I see a business with a good board of directors, I know that a man has a business which will continue. It is a very reliable indicator and, for my money, a basic requirement.

In my own experience, I find that on my board of directors, as well as in my personal life, the man who helps me the most is not the man who tells me something I don't know, but the man in whose presence I am provoked to think more soundly about things I do know but overlook. He will bring insight to bear on the things that I have not looked at in quite his way. When he points his finger at my mistakes, it hurts. Some people provoke thought; some just irritate; others make a man want to cry in his cups. A good board member won't make the boss feel sorry for himself; he will offer the owner a mental "tonic," a solution, however bitter. These people are rare. The fewer people the chief executive knows, the less chance he has of finding them for his board.

The president must look for people who are worthy of trust . . . people esteemed professionally and ethically; people who are interested in contributing; people who are able to enlarge present concepts of management; successful people with good reputations; people with courage, confidence, and curiosity; questioners, not listeners. He should stay away from those that are hostile or ignorant. Buck passers or "yes men" are of no service.

By participation in seminars and by serving on boards of local business, civic and charitable organizations, company presidents can become acquainted with their peers in a problem-solving situation, and thus reduce their parochialism. Because they have had an opportunity to know, understand and respect each other in mutual problem solving, we have found that many participants in our Institute's Invitational Seminars later seek each other out for board memberships. One word of warning, however. Though board members are naturally enriched by other memberships, too many such memberships will dilute their effectiveness. Three or four memberships would seem to be as many as one man can handle really well.

3. *How Many People Does A Board Need and How Long Should They Serve?* Too many members on the board restricts its effectiveness; too few limits its diversity. The actual number of directors is an individual requirement which must be worked out by the chief executive as chairman. In general, the more people on the board, the better, up to the point at which participation becomes difficult. There should be enough members to provide diversity. Five is much better than three; but more than eight or nine is usually too cumbersome to be effective. The size, complexity, and needs of the firm, however, are the determining factors.

I like the number five. I don't specify the number five because it's an odd number. It's just that I believe five to be a good, manageable number. Too many more people increase the chance of having a mass harangue instead of a board meeting. Any less than that, and, if some are missing, you can't even have a good bridge game. So I'd pick three outside members who should have absolutely no relationship to the company and should ideally join the board together for maximum total mutual reinforcement. If insiders number more than two, increase the number of outsiders to provide balance.

Whatever the total number of members, the most important factor is that there should be as much mixture as possible in all areas; backgrounds, businesses, ages, and special talents. While any closely held company may differ from others in the nature of its specific products, markets, and management styles, most of its problems are faced by other businesses, and the people who will best understand the owner president and his goals are other such businessmen.

Tenure on the board is not for life. One of the first duties of the formal board should be to set a policy of membership tenure so that non re-election later does not become a personal matter. After three or four years on a board, members get type-cast and their utility diminishes. Also, new members provide new insights and keep the president/owner stimulated to articulate his basic concepts. The retiring director should be responsible for initiating the search for his replacement, but the final decision must remain with the owner.

4. *Are Board Members Paid?* Although no owner can hope to compensate at true value the service that top notch board members will provide, compensation is mandatory for a man of this calibre who offers his time and thought as a director. Obviously, the quality of this man's contribution is not influenced by the amount of money he is paid, especially from a man whose opinion is not normally for sale and whose contribution to the president is non-purchasable. Payment, however, impels both the recipient and the donor to make special efforts to justify the explicit assumption of mutual responsibility.

Some company presidents think that paying $50-$100 per meeting is good enough. It isn't. Nobody is impressed by these amounts nor feels especially responsible. Directors should be paid a yearly retainer, irrespective of attendance, and they'll be sure to show up. Their pride will see to that. Two to three thousand dollars per annum is not too much to offer the members of the Board. At that price, the president will prepare himself well so that the meetings are not a waste of time and will listen to what is said. For this amount, directors realize that the president-owner is serious, and they'll not willingly disappoint him by non-attendance, non preparation or superficial thinking. They want to be considered worthy of their responsibility and consideration.

5. *Why Should Anyone Accept a Directorship in a Company?* Men accept directorships for a variety of reasons. If the owner has built a company which enjoys the respect of its suppliers, customers, and competitors, then service on his board of directors should be a matter of both pride and challenge for the man invited to so serve. In some cases, a man agrees to serve on another man's board for the stimulation it offers. Many executives find that serving on the boards of other companies increases their own knowledge and understanding, and they become better managers of their own companies. And, finally, many men have enjoyed a good and noble life from their experience in the world of business. One way of repaying the debt they feel to those that aided them in their quests, is to provide their time, service, energy, and commitment to insure the survival and growth of the dreams of others and thus, to make the world of business a continually better world. They've had good and successful lives, and they wish to give something back in return.

Compensation is rarely a factor in the acceptance of a directorship. The men who accept them rarely need the money, and there is no way to compensate these men for what they have to offer. In the privately held business, where ownership of shares in the company offers little value in terms of dividends or return on investment, ownership in the firm is not a reason for board membership and an offer of token shareholding is of dubious value.

Just as all the girls a man asks to marry him do not accept, all those asked to be directors may not necessarily accept. Some men quite honestly feel that they cannot afford the time required for preparation and attendance at meetings. Others may feel that service on some boards would create a conflict of interest, put them in a position of self-gain, or competitive advantage. Also, if a man has any question as to the character, reputation, or stability of the inviting company or its management, he will decline the invitation. He would only be a detriment to the company if he disapproves of its business policies, believes that its management is incompetent or in an unnecessary state of flux, or suspects that the company is on the verge of disaster for whatever reason. Sometimes good men refuse board directorships for fear of the personal liability involved in suits against the company. This can usually be minimized through a written "hold harmless" clause in the company by-laws as well as by purchasing insurance protection against director's liability.

6. *What Are Some of the Responsibilities of the Directors?* The legal duties of members of the board of directors are spelled out by law and should be well known to every company attorney. In addition to the usual boiler plate requirements with respect to compensation, dividends, election of officers and capital authorization, the law in most states indicates that the board of directors must:

a)　Exercise the same judgment and care in directing the company that any businessman would show in similar circumstances including the direct questioning of actions of the company which he feels are improper, and

b)　Refrain from taking specific actions as a member of the board which would by intention result in his own personal gain.

Although these legal duties permit wide interpretation, there are numerous extra-legal functions of the board member which are of particular importance in the family owned company. The board can be a major asset to a private company as a legitimate pressure group on the president. The president has no one who knows enough about his company to really put a burr under his saddle. In its function as the watchdog of management, the board is the devil's advocate, the embarrassing questioner. It keeps a wary eye on management and asks searching questions at the right time.

The board acts as both the tester and the grader of management. It sets time limits on goals to create pressure for action. It must be able to analyze and isolate the truth without being polite. In this way it will create a self-conscious management of the highest order. There are lots of people who "bug" the head of a company, but they are just professional irritants. A director is a man who respects the chief executive as a person, who likes him and wants him to succeed, but who also wants him to keep trying harder and harder.

This is the kind of man with whom the president must be perfectly honest and for whose directorship he must strive constantly to be worthy.

In addition to the fulfillment of legal obligations, there are at least five other kinds of support which a board member can offer to the president of the company:

1) *communication* of his understanding and awareness of that elusive state of affairs known as "general business conditions,"

2) *sharing* of his distinct personal professional skills;

3) *guidance* in developing, communicating, and implementing company policy; and

4) *guidance* at times of crisis in developing strategies for dealing with the problems.

The single most important job of the board of directors in the family corporation should be its *fifth* task—*to provide for the profitable continuity of the firm*. It must promote proper management development to allow for the "passing of the torch" from the founder generation to the successor generation. It must help bridge the generation gap and the attendant problems in communicating goals to the young and assuring the competence of the successor.

When the incumbent president retires or dies, the new president should have a working board to help him. If the board is familiar with past corporate policies and has been actively engaged in planning and measuring performance against these plans, it can give a great deal of assistance to the successor management team. The board is a policy setter, not an after-the-fact operation, but an entity with a definite, articulated line of policy on corporate issues.

The board must be an innovative group in the area of growth. It should challenge the imagination of management and stimulate fresh outlook—spark new thinking, not just review the old. "Innovation" does not consist of wild ideas but of well thought-out concepts in keeping with the needs and opportunities of the real world. Some businesses have come to their stagnation point. They have zero ideas. Their managers wait for the mail to come in to have something to do. Other companies have more good ideas than Congress has bills.

A working, virile board of directors can be a major asset to an owner-managed company in spurring new ideas and development by placing pressure on the president to set goals, timetables, and responsibilities. It can offer constructive objectivity in the complex "father/son, boss/employee" relationship. It can be a vehicle to retire a father who won't quit, and also to pressure a founder into training his successor. Although Dad equates survival with success, the board knows he is wrong. He is mostly just treading water. A board of directors committed to a man they esteem and respect can help him see the true danger of this state of affairs before he drowns not only himself, but all those who have attached themselves to him.

7. *How Should An Owner Work With His Board?* The chairman of the board of directors should be the incumbent president. As chairman, it is his duty to preside at meetings and to make them of optimum value. He must formalize the number of meetings, their length, their location, and their agenda. The board should meet periodically, if it is to contribute significantly to the operation, at least four times a year and at regularly scheduled intervals. For example, the first Monday after the quarterly financial statements can be made available. Meetings held more often than that would be too frequent, and meeting less than that is the same as doing nothing at all.

Quarterly meetings planned to last a minimum of a half day are best, scheduled in the morning. People tend to lose their steam after a drink at lunch. In addition, it's tough for a man to be at his best at an important afternoon meeting after already having fought one war in the morning. Morning board meetings are also preferable because they tend to provide a reservoir of time in case something unexpected comes up and needs to be explored. If meetings are scheduled to end at 5 pm, people start becoming agitated at quarter to five because they want to catch a plane, get home, or make a dinner party. Once the president has decided how often the board will meet and who will be on the board, he should pick fixed meeting dates for the whole year. It's foolish to wonder, "When are we going to get together again?"

In keeping with the seriousness of the board's responsibilities and the contribution expected of its members and its consideration of corporate policy rather than operational matters, it is not necessary that all meetings be held at the home office. Of the four meetings per year, most should be held at the plant, and can include a tour to keep members up-to-date on the physical changes and improvements to facilities and processes. Other meetings can be held at non-company locations in keeping with the dignity and the station of the members and the importance of the matters to be discussed. A working atmosphere should be preeminent. (Managers and employees are impressed when the board members arrive in the company office.) Minutes should be concise, to the point, and reflect accurately the ideas expressed, both pro and con. A reminder, in the minutes, of the spirit as well as the substance of discussion and decision is helpful to all directors in planning for future meetings.

In addition to being prime mover and moderator, the chairman must listen. This is not just an instance of a good captive audience for his elaborate comments about his own company. His board is there to advise him, as well as for him to report to them. Therefore, one of the most important factors to consider in making the meeting successful is the preparation of a planned, written agenda. It should be mailed in advance to members of the board. It should be accompanied by documents and materials to give the members the necessary information to enable them to make well thought-out decisions without creating such a deluge of paper that it is ignored.

One of the greatest problems a director faces is acquiring enough accurate information about the company to enable him to participate in intelligent discussion and make intelligent decisions. To get his "money's worth" from a director, a president must make certain that he provides him with information which is timely and exposes the director to company operations and personnel as well as policy. He should indicate what things he feels he is doing correctly both in preparing his future plans and in carrying out his present activities. There are times when this may require a great pile of papers to support the points prepared for the directors. To assist the directors in digesting the material, the president/chairman may want to prepare a brief outline and identify the material accompanying it as exhibits.

Both the preparation of the agenda and the accompanying supportive material are the responsibility of the chairman. For conscientious directors, the absorption of such valid information is of utmost importance. Over a continuing period, it can provide them with a profile of the development of the company and may offer clues to questions which should be asked—questions which the president either may not see or is unwilling to ask himself. A director cannot act as counsel and consultant to the president, if the president does not help him to understand the company's past, its present, and his hopes for its future.

In addition to information prepared for the quarterly meeting, there should be periodic reports between meetings to keep board members up to date. No one can argue with the president in his own business unless he reveals to them the information they need to have in order to be able to question him intelligently. When Board members are not prepared, it is because the president hasn't given them information. They come to a meeting without any knowledge of what is going to be discussed. In a situation such as this, they are not in a position to be very helpful since no homework preceded their attendance at the meeting. Worthwhile opinions cannot usually be given off the cuff. Don't make speed readers out of directors by giving them data just as the meeting starts.

The distribution of information is a very touchy subject in closely-held companies. The amount of information given out depends on how "secure" the president feels in his own business. Actually, there is no point in his worrying about the past; it is the future he must try to protect. Invariably, presidents who need protection the least, share information the most. Those who need help the most, share their information the least. This is the nature of the species. The more inbred the company, the more fearful it is. Some misguided chief executives will even try deliberately to mis-state the facts to their directors in order that their own actions not be questioned. This is both a dishonest and unintelligent approach. If a man has good directors, this is not the way to make the most of their success. The board cannot be treated as a high-priced decoration or sterile status symbol. In order to contribute to the well-being of any company, competent board members will demand to be kept well informed at all times of all important policy considerations. They will expect to receive financial and other data bearing on the overall performance of the company both with respect to the short and the long range goals and objectives they helped establish.

A board of directors properly selected and imbued with real authority for review of the president provides a major thrust in the process of involving the business owner in auditing his decisions and actions. If the board has an active interest in the success of the business, it will not sit back and allow the owner to continue arbitrary and non-productive policies without questioning these policies and suggesting alternatives. Such an outside objective review of the kinds of decisions and actions which the owner has made is an invaluable aid in improving his own managerial ability. Furthermore, by providing him a sounding board for reviewing his ideas before he puts them into action, the board offers the president an instrument for maximizing his options. It has the ability to support his ideas or offer alternatives for his consideration thus enlarging his view and the choice of action open to him.

The president should welcome a board willing to become his active ally and protagonist. He does not want and cannot use a rubber stamp, uninvolved board. He must say to his directors, as the boy said to the girl, "I'm not interested in your tacit acquiescence. I want your active participation."

Chapter Nine

Managing Succession

CHOICE NOT CHANCE

The business owner who has seen his company flourish under his own hands must not forego the burden of leadership when the going gets rough. He must make the tough decisions as well as the easy ones and one of the toughest decisions he must make is planning for the future of his business through the coming generations. Whether he likes it or not, his business must someday run without him.

Far too many owners hang onto their business control into senility, and by the time, if ever, that they do get around to thinking about succession, their heirs may no longer be interested or competent in continuing the company. They may have entered another field, or moved to the other end of the country or adjusted to the requirements of mediocrity—because that is all that has been asked of them. What are the alternatives then open to the owner? How can he pass the company on, as he himself inevitably deteriorates over time? Who will want it, then?

143

A man who won't train his successor is a man who won't accept replacement. He thinks he can always find a buyer who will offer him an employment contract. Such a buyer, if found, would very probably under such circumstances deduct from the purchase price an amount equal to the salary he would plan to pay the previous owner over the years of service anticipated. This just kids the owner manager into the belief that he's wanted. It makes him feel happy. As soon as he puts his signature to the purchase agreement, however, requests for his management contribution will be zero. The new owner would like to mail his check to him in Zanzibar.

Seventy-five year olds won't believe me at all, but I hope anyone reading this at age 30 will get more out of it than he would at 40, because he'll be watching the old replay prior to the start of his own game. Forty-year-olds will get more than the 50's; 50's will get more than the 60's; and I hope 60 year-olds will realize they better get off the dime.

The business owner cannot procrastinate about choosing his successor. He must plan for the continuity of his business if it is his hope or wish that it continue, and not depend upon chance events or divine intervention to provide a successor for him. He cannot nor should he try to keep his choice of successor a secret. Continuity of the family company is the justification for nepotism. I do not mean blind, untrained, irresponsible, immature nepotism. I mean planned, trained, and responsible nepotism. *Whoever the nepot is—family or non family—*this takes planning and faith, and guts.

The future president of the company twenty years from now, assuming the company is still in business at that time, should be a matter of choice and training, not luck. No business owner has enough competent people working for him to leave succession to chance. If he is fortunate enough to have a few good managers by blood or recruitment, he is multi-blessed. His choice of a successor must be based on the needs of the company for the future, not a replay of the requirements of the past. The choice must take into account how the business needs to be run tomorrow. The man who replaces the business owner must be trained to think in both present and future terms. Consequently, I make a strong plea that business owners really become the selectors of their successors rather than compensators for the inadequacies of their subordinates. For most business owners, this choice will involve a son.

NEPOTISM ISN'T ALWAYS BAD

Monarchies were, in concept, family corporations, but royal successors were never in doubt. The first male heir was the crown prince. The laws of primogeniture were well established. The only problem occurred when by war or disease or accident, the king died before the young prince was physically able to take charge. Enter the regent—the executive vice president of the monarchy—the brother of the king or the old counselor who, but for the little prince, would now have been king himself. The regent probably considered himself well-qualified. What usually happened to the little prince during the inter-regnum? He usually got poisoned, poor kid. The job benefits were too attractive to give away to someone who hadn't earned it or worked to become qualified for it. Too often the regent or the executive vice president or Rasputin, the ambitious advisor, react the same way; the parallels are all too true.

The family business must have an heir. The responsibility for choosing an heir is up to Dad. He is the king and must accept this duty to choose his successor. It simplifies things if well-prepared, well-motivated sons choose to take on the mantle, but some sons have no interest in their father's business. Forcing them to succeed to the office can only be a disaster. It would be far wiser to let the son go to work elsewhere—as an archeologist in Afghanistan or a dentist in Detroit—than to force him to be a manager, if managing is not his talent. But you have to face up to it.

Hard as it may be to accept, in reality, some sons genuinely don't have any interest or aptitude for their father's business. The owner should not let his business become a holding pattern for uncertainty or a prison to be escaped from after his departure. It ruins the sense of mutual participation and accomplishment on the part of other employees and managers in his company, who really do enjoy their work and the satisfaction it gives them. The attitude of unmotivated sons in Dad's business can create a disastrous management atmosphere for the future. It is better to let sons follow their own pursuits and let successors be chosen from those who willingly accept the challenge offered.

Nepotism is the only way an owner-managed business will survive. It just depends on who is designated the nepot. Believe it or not, sons-in-laws make good potential heirs. They did not grow up believing they were going to inherit a business so they may really have prepared themselves to work for a living. Their candidacy occurs because they happened to marry a fine girl and to be in the right place when a company needed a successor. Where no family relation exists to continue the business, the boss may have corporate sons, adopted sons so to speak, in those managers whom he has raised and trained in the business, who can become his business heirs. There are many possibilities, but the choice must be made.

The choice of successor determines the mechanics of passing on both the owner's knowledge and his business. The business owner must have an urge to leave something meaningful behind, however, or the mechanics are meaningless. Most men want to be remembered as philanthropists and not as Philistines. Therefore, most business owners hope that they will be remembered and honored for the works they leave behind. Because only those who own the business must face the full implications of successor management, they must understand the requirements of seeking a successor. They must, in the fullness of their life, make their choice and announce it to all whose acceptance is necessary to the perpetuation of the business.

THE BUSINESS OWNER AS TEACHER

The business owner must become a teacher. He must realize that both teachers and businessmen have the same responsibility, to pass their knowledge on to those who will succeed them. If the businessman can't teach what he knows to those who will follow him, then he'll continue doing everything all by himself until he drops. What he built during his lifetime will be destroyed. To "work" or to "teach" is a personal choice. He must make the decision; but it's a sad situation for a man to place himself in the position of "semi-retirement" while everyone else is waiting for him to disappear. The greatest retirement role for the businessman is as a teacher, not standing in front of a class expounding his management techniques, but as a teacher in his own university explaining his own business.

The older he gets, the fewer options the owner manager has. Usually, fathers have their children in their 20's and 30's. Usually they have all the children they're going to have by age 40. By 40-45 presidents have to realize that they have a finite family and a 20 year period in which to select and train a chosen heir. If a man waits until he is 67 to realize he must teach his 40 year old son, he's waited 20 years too long and the class is over, before it starts. This owner has lost. He has no options left. Like the fisherman who eats his own bait, his fishing days will be soon over.

Where does the businessman-teacher get the perspective or judgment that allows him to teach? Most presidents have not had, since the day they assumed office, any real requirement to "sell" the opinions that they "buy." They just stand up there and state them and expect their audience to nod their heads dutifully without question or suggestion. Those who disagree can do as they please or leave and work elsewhere. In their success, these owner managers have created a built-in agreement system for their bias, right or wrong. Unlike a good teacher who keeps up with new opinions in his field, the business owner is too often content to rely on what he already knows and expects the same response from his employees.

A teacher who considers himself omniscient, however, is in real trouble. He will soon fail. He may have tenure in his lifetime and his opinions may be unchallenged in his classroom, but the students in his class will sooner or later say, "he failed us." Here again is where the absence of a board of directors is a great disservice to the business owner, because he has nobody to grade him or his efforts. He gives himself an "A" because he pays the bills. But to continue to succeed, he will have to find someone who will grade him objectively and whose grades he will accept. It isn't easy.

The business owner knows he must train his successor and to do this well he needs a board of directors who'll review his progress in that training and insist that he graduate his student. He also needs a council of advisors who will help him fill in the gaps in the curriculum where he doesn't know the subject matter.

It's rough on the business owner who is really serious about preparing a competent successor to take his place. He has to establish his own school, compete for the students, fund his own scholarships, develop his own curriculum and pick his own faculty. Then he has to allow these others to examine his own grasp of the curriculum so that he, in turn, can see that this body of knowledge is passed on to his successors and made relevant to their future.

He, himself, must set the date for graduation or his university will not encourage good students to attend or motivate them to learn. An incumbent president cannot keep his successors in a perpetual role of "understudy" awaiting a chance to "go on." Without requiring for graduation that the student be "smarter" than his teachers, the president must say, "My son, you must now assume your ultimate responsibility" and graduate his heir from the job of "son" to the job of chief executive officer. He can't ask God to set the date by having him hit by the proverbial truck.

NOTHING SUBSTITUTES FOR THE OWNER'S COMMITMENT AND ENTHUSIASM

What the family business needs is not for the owner to get smarter and smarter and to work harder and harder at what he's already been doing all these years, but for him to make a continuing major commitment and investment of his time in preparing his successor for the future responsibility of his inheritance.

In addition to investing this time with his successor, he must, from an early age, share his enthusiasm with the heir whom he hopes will follow in his footsteps. Business interest is usually aroused in children by their fathers at an early age through dad's enthusiasm for his work, its risks, challenges and satisfactions, the happiness and rewards it provides him and his family, and through the interesting people children meet through their association with their father.

The owner managed business is not all hell made liveable by martinis. Dad does his son no service if he lets him think so. Kids are very vulnerable to the attitudes of adults, and when Dad tries to change at 20 the attitude he inspired in his son at 10, he's going to find the going very rough. Dad must express the same enthusiasm for his work as do swim coaches, commercial pilots, science teachers, or skiing photographers. These men exude a feeling of joy and social contribution. Imagine how many youngsters would be interested in flying as a career if all they heard about it were the engine failures, the thunderstorms, the instrument malfunctions, and the near misses. That's mostly what they hear about business at home—the tremendous problems and irritations the old man has to face.

It is the job of the father of a 16-year-old who hopes to attract his son into his business to make the business itself attractive. At 16, few young men know what business is all about. They think business is like the family car to be used for their own enjoyment, or they think business is long lunches, authority without responsibility, squabbles over money and/or jobs by members of the family and privilege by status not competence. Either view really contradicts their sense of ethic. A potential successor needs to see the successes, the failures, the dreams, the privileges which stem from accomplishment, the opportunities for innovation, and the great feeling of fulfillment the company provides in order to understand the world of business in its total perspective.

What usually happens, however, is that the boss is so busy climbing the ladder of economic success he hardly sees the poor kids as they grow up. So, after they turn 8 or 9, he takes them to the office to keep him company on Saturdays and impress them with how hard he works. While Dad reads the mail and attends to business, he leaves the little fellow with the foreman and says, "Sam, take care of the kid." So Sam lets the kid mix up all the nuts and bolts, sort through the scrap barrel, rearrange the labels in the shipping room, push the buttons on everything he can find in the office and irritate the hell out of all the people who have to straighten up after him. The company is a big playpen with an adult nurse called a foreman. In this way the boss has unwittingly begun the process of making his son feel that company employees are his personal domestics, and that the plant and the office are his inherited sandboxes. No wonder the owner manager often resents the attitude of his son in later life. If he is honest with himself, he helped to create the attitude.

The owner manager adds to his son's misconceptions as the boy gets older by providing meaningless summer employment on an adult wage scale which the youngster doesn't understand. The boss needs someone to mow the office lawn, paint stripes in the parking lot, or wash the shop windows, and he pays the kid the going wage, which is more money than the boy ever saw in his life for no more work than he does to earn his allowance. Now by 16-18 the business has become for the boy not only a playpen but a system to exploit. To him it's meaningless labor of unimportant quality for high profit.

After a couple of summers like this the lad goes off to college and works in between semesters at additional jobs of an unspecified and ungraded quality. The son is secure in knowing that he will not be reproached and is invincible against being fired. Dad now finds he can get even with the IRS by having his son's allowance subsidized by the government by calling it salary. If he can make his son Assistant Secretary of the company as a high school graduation present, he may even be able to get the funds out of his business to pay the young man's college education. Then he can top it off with a guaranteed job as Vice President—Custodial Services (janitor) when the boy gets out of college. No wonder so many children grow up thinking business is a combination of executive sandbox and a license to cheat the government. With this kind of introduction to the world of business, by the time they graduate they have a lopsided view of business activity which it will take a lifetime to erase. Being a father is hard enough . . . but being a father of a successor is even harder. It demands time, enthusiasm, and constant surveillance.

It's not easy being this man's son, either. But if they hope to become heirs to the toils and teachings of their father, smart students learn to exhibit enthusiasm for their professors and their professor's accomplishments—eager students do a great deal to inspire the teacher to want to be understood. Smart students who want to learn don't start off by breathing onions on the professor. Boys can learn good lessons about business at an early age by summer work and their early pay-checks; where the money comes from, the amount of time it takes to produce it, what it will provide, and how far it will go. Dad's going to give him a job and the money some day. Why not let him begin to learn early about work and fiscal discipline. Like athletic discipline, it can be a subject of personal pride; it usually depends on the coach.

Summer employment need not be token work at outlandish salaries or slave labor at slave wages. There are many tasks which a young man of high school and college age can perform with great competence. In many cases his contemporaries are doing them for a living. If a successor is to understand the nature of the business and the pressures on various work groups when he enters a company as a manager, he would do well to walk in the moccasins of a useful employee for awhile. What better way to get a feel for the various positions, the skills, and the responsibilities involved in the factory or field than by working in those areas himself? The business owner can, in effect, design a part-time management training program for his son while the young man is also completing his formal education.

In most cases, such programs when constructed in the family business itself are badly done and only serve to alienate the son, infuriate the non-family management and create personality conflicts between the son and future subordinates which may never die. Simply to thrust his son off on a series of managers, each getting "the kid" for a week, without any kind of preparation or understanding of the reasons behind this move, is to invite disaster. The owner who really wishes to prepare his successor will have his son find work in other than Dad's business. Most mothers unfortunately won't buy this idea—they want their boy to enjoy the fruits of a father's labor he doesn't yet appreciate.

In college, the business owner should not discourage his son from pursuing whatever area of knowledge interests him—the broader the education, the better. For too many students, "business administration" is a worthless trip through an overgrown jungle of obsolete or useless opinion perpetrated by those who rarely practice what they teach in a real business situation. Without intervening work experience, graduate business schools are too often additional years of the same. It would be much better for a boy to take courses in anthropology or music or foreign languages, if that is how he will best commit his energies to think, and plan, and make judgments on his own. Moreover, most teachers in these fields have an enthusiasm for their subject which business educators could wisely emulate in the motivation of students. A good teacher in school can prepare a son to seek good teachers in the business world instead of encouraging cynicism and criticism.

ENCOURAGE A SON TO WORK ELSEWHERE FIRST

To offer employment in the family business to the heir right out of school is a bad idea. It gives him an exaggerated view of his value, either too high or too low, and provides few opportunities for testing. If he works only for his Dad, all that the son learns is what Dad tells him or lets him see. It offers him no new experience, no new skills, no new associations, no place to learn true initiative or to accept the just effects of error. Once he is on the company payroll full time, it is almost impossible for him to leave. He is in a terminal position. Like marrying too young, this move too often leads to regrets or infidelity.

If the poor fellow is single, and lives at home, and works for his father, he really has problems. There is no distinction between life at home and life at the office. Dad at dinner is Dad at the office. Momma in the kitchen may also be treasurer at the office and the repository of the secrets of the corporate boudoir. She certainly gets unduly involved. Business gossip becomes the after-hours agenda at home, where he is hopelessly enmeshed, usually with regrettable repercussions.

BROADEN A SUCCESSOR('S) EXPERIENCE

A son should learn about business elsewhere where he can make his mistakes and not embarrass his father, and where his early uncertainties and ignorance won't cast doubt on his ability as a manager in the years to come. If he has had no outside experience but comes from school directly into the family business, there is no way that he could have had an opportunity to earn his spurs and test himself to his own satisfaction. He will be forever left with that nagging fear, "Could I have made it on my own?"

Perhaps he can enter the training program of one of the company's suppliers or a publicly owned company in a related field, or Dad may be able to work out an arrangement with another business owner to provide meaningful employment for their mutual heirs. At any rate, this owner should encourage his son to work for someone else for 3-4-5 or even 10 years, if he can, to get varied business experience and *managerial success* before he joins the family firm permanently. In this way, he can learn what kind of stuff he's made of without help from instructors who either give him the answers for all the tests or ignore his failing performance. This is where he should get his industrial undergraduate experience.

The business owner father is really best for providing the graduate business specialization required for working in his specific custom-built company. If a son enters his dad's graduate industrial program immediately out of school, he lacks the basic pre-requisites provided by prior experience elsewhere to appreciate the things Dad does "differently" or to understand why, and when to suggest change, or when to resist change.

Business, society and technology have grown much more complicated since Dad built the firm. The son needs to have both experience, confidence and perspective on the alternative open to him for his success in the future.

WORKING FOR THE FAMILY BUSINESS

If, however, a young man must for special reasons go to work with his father right after college, he should be given employment and hired on the same basis as an outsider. No cute nicknames, no calling him "son," and no letting him call the boss "Dad." It only serves to emphasize his uniqueness, and he doesn't want it at that stage. No weekday lunches at the club with Dad, no special favors which the boss doesn't do for anyone else in the same job. The poor guy wants to cut it on his own, and his father won't let him. He wants to be a good employee, and he really wants to earn his keep. He knows he is not really a manager of anything, even though, for pseudo-legal purposes, he may be listed on the letterhead as vice-president and secretary. It is not easy for a young man in his position.

A son wants to be on equal footing with his peers and contemporaries. He should be paid at the same rate as anyone else with the same qualifications, not less to make him tough, and not more because his salary is pretax. He may end up feeling more equal than he really wants to be having to compete for his jobs on the same basis as any other applicant, but that's good discipline. Unfortunately, most sons do not really get hired at the going rate. One of the hardest things for sons to understand, therefore, is that they are either overpaid or underpaid for what they do. Most could not or would not hold a job elsewhere at the same pay. They should be able to sell what they know in the marketplace for the same amount of money they get in Dad's firm. If they get more, then shareholder dividends are being included in their salary and they ought to know it. If they get less, they are being discriminated against and they deserve a raise.

Now let us suppose that a son has become a qualified manager in the company. When he works for Dad as a manager, there should be a real job for him to fill with clear cut responsibilities and definable successes. Dad must think of himself as a teacher who is learning along with his best student, and not be too quick to veto the young man's ideas or cover up his inadequacies. One of the saddest cases I've seen recently involved the founder of a metal extruding firm and his middle-aged son, a graduate engineer. Old Dad is now 73 and he has worked hard at the business all of his adult life, and he has virtually built the small town in which his plant flourishes. He controls the largest payroll in the area. Until recently the company has suffered few layoffs and job mobility among his employees was low; their product was highly respected and in great demand. It would seem that here was a business any son would be proud to inherit.

Twenty five years ago, that may have been the case. Fresh out of engineering school and after four years with the Army engineers, the heir joined the company eager to prove himself worthy of his potential inheritance. Brash but bright, he designed a new system for forming metal which could have cut considerable operating time and consequently reduced total costs. Although implementing the system would have required workers with more specialized job skills, the higher salary rates incurred would have been equalized by the concurrent elimination of many unskilled jobs.

But before the young man had an opportunity to fully explain to his father his concepts and his plans for offering the necessary training to company employees, word about the new program spread rapidly through the plant.

The spectre of layoffs and job loss caused widespread reaction especially among the unskilled labor. The father feared that the first major strike in company history loomed on the horizon. Rather than listen to a careful explanation of the new methods, Dad chose to quell the strike threat by demolishing his son's plans with the ringing injunction, "Don't ever practice your damn fool ideas with my money."

From then on, any attempt by the son to explain or to suggest further new ideas brought from the old man continuing rebukes and pungent reminders of the near disaster which his son's "mistake" had nearly cost the company. Employees, aware of how and why "the boss" had personally squelched the plan, now knew how to undermine any attempts at leadership by the son by keeping everyone in the front office informed of "junior's interference" in the operations of the business. The young man even tried to set up his own R&D department to justify his salary, but there emerged little research and no development. Rebuffed on all sides at any attempt to apply his engineering skills in modernizing the business, the successor realized that he would never have his father's confidence. Now, at 50, although he is still listed as "Vice President of Research and Development," he is active mostly at the country club bar. Dad may someday be ready to get out of the business, but he has not allowed anyone else to learn to manage it.

Don't dismiss this story as unique. It isn't. The sad fact is that in far too many cases, this story is duplicated over and over again in every part of the country in almost every industry. Too many fathers kill off the ability and creativity of a competent heir the first time the son advances a new idea. And if he doesn't give up the first time, the poor kid will get knocked down two or three times. After awhile he'll quit getting up for the next round. And then, when Dad finally discovers that he really does need help, he wonders why there is no successor ready to step in and lend a hand.

As his son progresses in the company the business owner must discipline himself to listen to his successor's ideas and risk trying some of them. We all learn far more from our failures than we do from our successes. The young man must be permitted to manage his plans and put them into effect; he must see the results of his errors, and his father's errors, and he must be allowed the responsibility of choosing his contemporaries to help him manage. The business owner must make it clear to all whom he has chosen as his successor, and the owner must clean out his own dead wood; he put it there. The owner manager can't arbitrarily resist the changes in method, processes and attitude his successor brings to his job. The successor needs to operate as himself, not as the bosses' understudy, double, alter-ego, or replayed youth.

The business owner should act like a pro and treat his son like a pro. He should avoid the temptation of giving him vague or dummy titles. The successor deserves a line job. That's what he really wants. He needs to understand how the business operates and be able to influence this operation. Athletics teaches a young man that the pros are organized, that they know what they are doing. The players have specific assignments; the plays are worked out in advance; there is cooperation among all the members of the team; they accept the coach as understanding, qualified, and impartial. Too often the son who goes into his dad's business is disappointed because he can't see the organization, understand the plays, evaluate the players or watch the replay. He doesn't even know the rules, or who makes them or who changes them. It's Dad's job to make things clear so that his son understands how things happen in the family company's game plan.

At this juncture, the position of the founder and successor must be that of teacher and student. The founder must treat his son like an employee who is going to succeed in the business. He must set standards of interim accomplishments, to measure progress. The successor can't go from "in charge of the annual company picnic" to "executive vice president." Neither should he be a perpetual "assistant to the president"—the fire fighter's fire fighter in charge of little fires.

One excellent way for a father to help teach his son his particular business is through an understanding of finance. This does not mean the bookkeeper's figures. I mean the philosophy of financial analysis, the concept of profit centers, of capital equipment justification, of allocation of labor cost, of planning, of forecasting, of budgeting, controlling and evaluating.

Owner managers must learn to allow the next-in-line to make mistakes, if necessary. His mistake might result in a loss of $1,000 or $10,000 or more, but in the long run, it could be the cheapest mistake the company ever made, because the lesson may temper or avoid disastrous decisions later on. Business is somewhat like a parachute jump: it's not the long, slow fall that hurts; it's the short, fast stop.

As the company grows older, the founder must become more and more of a teacher and less of a doer. He must not compensate for the inadequacies of his own subordinates, including his successor. It is especially difficult for a founder to quit "doing" because he can do just about any job in the plant quicker and better than anyone else; but he has to learn to let go. He cannot manipulate his tenure to keep his son down.

TENURE DOES NOT IMPLY COMPETENCE

Tenure is not limited just to teachers and bureaucrats. Owner managers get tenure, too. They get it because they are lord and master of their own empire and they decree tenure upon themselves. Their decision to award tenure, however unconscious it may be, is never subject to review, and is binding for life. Only death or the decision to abdicate ends this tenure.

The tenure of the owner manager is even more lasting than that of a school teacher or bureaucrat. A teacher's tenure may be cut short for a variety of reasons, a bureaucrat's when political administrations change. The owner manager's tenure is limited only by his health, his virility, and his ability to avoid Chapter 11. As long as the money keeps coming in, the owner manager can run the business forever without change or review. No one can force him to step down, retire, or quit. It doesn't matter that his experience is obsolete, that the world has changed, that the knowledge with which he started his company may be outdated after all this time. Nothing dictates the limit of tenure for the owner manager nor forces him to continue to learn, adapt, and change, nor requires him to prepare others to take his place nor even to face up to the inevitable fact that every one of us obsolesces and will be replaced. This may be the most difficult factor with which the business owner must cope because he confuses survivorship with talent. Being alive does not necessarily mean he is healthy. It just means he's not dead.

It's difficult, I admit, to think about personal obsolescence. I too have these thoughts. When do I become obsolete? Times will change and the time will come when I will find myself unable to react and adapt to change and the rate of change as I once did. My own dad remembers the time when, if people didn't walk there, they didn't go. Now he has seen men walk on the moon. In my own lifetime, I remember when the American Dream was a chicken in every pot, and a car in every garage. Chicken now comes "just heat and serve" and on the average two cars belong to every family. Credit cards have replaced cash, and two weeks in Europe is no longer a once-in-a-lifetime dream. I keep a photograph in my office which shows my father and me in uniform during The War. It seems like yesterday when I look at the photograph, now. However, I must realize that at age 50, I am my father, and my son is me. If the world has changed so dramatically for my generation, what will my son—and all the sons of owner managers—experience in their lifetime?

If the world is indeed turning so fast, changing so rapidly, what does this mean to the owner manager? For one thing, it means his skills are becoming obsolete faster and faster. He must accept this fact and prepare for it wisely and willingly. How does the tenured owner manager accept his obsolescence? How does he prepare for its inevitable coming—because it must come even to the greatest of us. Why should he prepare for it? Does anyone care whether his business succeeds, fails, ends, or endures?

THE CHOICE IS YOURS

It is important for us to realize that there are many who do care. Sons, wives, daughters, care; communities, employees, suppliers, care—a whole host of people who have an interest in the business as an investment or a place of employment do care. Yet, though they may care, they don't know how to help. They have no real awareness or appreciation of the problems—the demands and pressures on the owner manager—because he hasn't allowed them to enter his world. To let them know where it hurts, and then to let them help, is to find the solution. Only when he can make them understand his problems and accept their help, can he really begin charting his business securely into the future. That, after all, is the business owner's prize. He can leave behind something worthwhile. A sense of destiny imposes upon the man the fact that he must plan for this reality.

The more competent a man is in his chosen field, the more important it becomes that he plan for his own replacement. A working lifetime is not an infinite period of time—it's more like 500 months. Most people reading this book probably have less than half of it remaining and for too many, 100 months are all that is left of their prime. That isn't much time in which to make a conscious effort to leave behind what we know.

RENAISSANCE NOT RETIREMENT

Men need to have a sense of destiny. This is a sort of vanity in which the business owner rarely indulges himself. Deep down, this is what the family business is all about; to build a successful business is a self-chosen date with destiny. Perhaps this is why destiny should be called retirement . . . the planned destiny . . . the Renaissance.

Historically, the Renaissance was applied to a golden age of art and culture, a culmination of all which had preceded it in the history of man. In the working world, the owner's renaissance can also be a golden period in which he endows those who follow him with the accumulation of knowledge and concern that he has spent a lifetime acquiring. Through these others he can create an immortality. Instead of facing the demise of his business as the result of his own death, he can live to see the revitalization of his business through the successor he himself has chosen and trained. Instead of being forced into a retirement of pablum and sulphur baths, he may see his golden years as the fulfillment of his dream.

Retirement can be a renaissance. Perhaps I can best describe my concept of this renaissance by comparing grandmothers with mothers-in-law. Grandmothers can take great pride in the independent actions of their grown children whom they have so well reared; but mothers-in-law perpetually try to fix up the second time around what they mishandled the first time. They are really the same women. Their image is a result of their attitude.

I think the concept of retirement is equal to the concept of the grandmother. Grandmothers are not "retired" mothers. Instead grandmotherhood is the fulfillment of their lives. If a man can't raise his successors to follow his dream after his stewardship has ended . . . then I say he has failed.

A business owner should not be a mother-in-law to his business. He must choose his heir as early as possible and discuss the choice with his successor to be sure that he accepts the responsibility. Then, as far in advance as possible, the owner should inform all his employees that on a given date—an irrevocable commitment which he will not change or alter at whim—his successor will become the chief executive officer of the business. This move will clarify the time of succession and eliminate any take-over attempts by self-designated Richelieus. Finally, and most important, when he retires, the owner must stay retired. When he finally moves out of the mainstream, he must stay out; one farewell appearance is sufficient and all that a successor should have to endure.

As one son put it to me recently, "If Dad would relax, and just give me moral support, he's worth $85,000 a year to our company. If he insists on coming to the office to check on what I'm doing, he's only worth about $8,500."

Chapter Ten

Managing the Estate
and Sharing the Dream

A WIDOW IS WAITING

It is a daily miracle that there are any owner-managed businesses left in this world. So few owner managers make adequate plans for the continuity of their businesses that the Good Lord shows His kindness to them everyday by allowing their businesses to continue.

The chain of events is always the same: the top man drops dead and the bereaved widow is saddled not only with an intense emotional crisis, but with a business crisis as well. She is less prepared for the latter than she is for the former. She doesn't know anything about her husband's business; she doesn't know any of the firm's advisors, its board of directors, bankers, accountants or key employees. Most important, she has no idea what her husband's goals or wishes are, because for all these years he has operated on the theory of selective nondisclosure. She, more than anyone else, has been the major target for this secrecy. In most cases, however, a

161

temporary solution to the dilemma is found. Employees rally round the cause, auditors lend their support, suppliers pitch in to help save an important cog in their business operation. But usually at some point in time, the business stops operating profitably and is sold for a percentage on the dollar to avoid further loss.

No one ever plans for catastrophe, and no man ever plans on dying. But catastrophes occur and men die. Along with the grief and sorrow, wives of owner managers have to suffer the frustration and risk of managing an estate and a business they know nothing about.

Sometime after the funeral, the business is explained to the wife—or perhaps it would be more accurate to say that someone tries to explain the business to the wife. She is operating from a decided disadvantage. Not only is she ignorant of the day-to-day operations of the corporation, but she also has no knowledge of the relative abilities of the company's advisors and/or managers, the very people who are explaining its mysteries to her.

In too many cases, alas, these advisors are second-rate because the owner-manager would not face up to the inevitable. While he was alive, he was the all-powerful, the divine. He didn't think he needed competent advisors then. His widow pays the price for his shortsightedness.

A few weeks ago I had a call from a lady whom I'd met, some years earlier, at a convention where I had spoken and which she had been attending with her husband. I remembered her as a very gracious and charming woman with absolutely no interest in or understanding of her husband's wholesale business.

He was a big burly, handsome fellow with a convincing manner and the guts to drive a hard bargain, and over the years he built a substantial company, although he ran a one-man show. His beautiful wife was his pride and joy, and he never troubled her with "business talk." She had never worked a day in her life and had no idea of the difference between accounts payable and accounts receivable. She enjoyed the results of her husband's labor, although she grumbled a bit about the amount of time he spent on the job. I even remember she had asked me at one of the coffee breaks, if I didn't think that a man who owned a business as successful as her husband's should spend more time at home and confine his working time to office hours.

As I said, I got a call from this lady only a few weeks ago. I wish that I hadn't. Her strong, healthy and wealthy husband had just suffered a fatal heart attack, and she was left as major stockholder, manager, and prime successor to the business. "What do I do now?" she asked.

How can I answer a question like that? Do I tell her to run it? Who knows what her husband did? Do I tell her to close up and call in the liquidators? Should she put the business on the market and try to find a buyer ... or what? What do you tell a woman whose husband thought he was immortal and never made any plans for the perpetuation of his business. What options did she really have ... and how much time ... and whom can she trust?

How does an owner-manager plan for his eventual departure from this world? In my experience, most business owners plan for that unhappy event in much the same way as they plan for their retirement never. Retirement and death are assumed to be one and the same thing. Retirement is nothing more than the removal of the owner manager from a position of authority within his lifetime—replacement on schedule.

The first thing the owner manager must do to forestall chaos at the time of his death is to sit down with his wife and have a long chat with her about what he does for a living, why he does it, and whose opinions he values and whose he doesn't trust. He should begin to do this as early in the life of the business as possible. These talks should be continued at least once a year to keep his wife acquainted with the current state of the business, including any plans for its future. He should explain to her where he thinks he is going with the business and at what relative point he is now.

This is not a once-in-lifetime event. It should be a continuing dialogue between husband and wife, but it has to start sometime. It must involve a meaningful discussion between them of the dreams, the goals, the visions and requirements involved in the manager's business and personal worlds. The owner must explain what the parts are, what the costs are, and what the rewards are likely to be. With an understanding wife and a bit of luck, the owner manager will be able to explain these dreams and goals. The owner manager must avoid the trap illustrated by the attitude "my business is different, my wife wouldn't understand." He is responsible for seeing that his wife does understand what his life's work is all about.

THE BUSINESS OWNER MUST SHARE HIS DREAM

Wives do not marry businessmen. They marry men. And, as such, they simply do not understand the pressures, priorities, and the trade-offs their husbands must make in order to be a successful owner of a family business. So the owner manager has a choice. He can either try to explain something to a wife who does not have the prerequisite background for understanding or, as happens in most cases, he can glibly say: "You wouldn't understand. Just pour me another drink."

But the wife hears something different. As her fur coat goes out of style and the kids teeth need orthodontia, a wife watches the man she loves wind himself tighter and tighter in order to supply these things at the same time that the business pressures mount. And she can't do anything about it because he won't let her. She doesn't know how to approach these problems. And at some point she says, "Stop. I don't want another fur; I don't want a bigger house, another club. Stop working so hard. Be a father. Be a husband." For my 47th birthday my wife gave me a five minute record of applause and a note that said, "Why don't you just stay home for awhile and talk to the children and me?" Success has got to mean applause at home.

The business owner lives in two worlds: one is his business; the other, his home. And the great tragedy is that his wife neither gets to see nor comes to know and understand or appreciate the former. That is her husband's great mistake. He must bring her into his business world and help her understand the pressures and trade-offs under which he operates. Otherwise, his total existence both at home and in the business will be in a shambles. Taking the time and the effort to begin to explain the world in which his business functions is a necessity towards not only a happier marriage, but also a more successful business.

I'm not advocating marriage counselling. That's a little out of my line. I'm talking, in this instance, about the relationship of the human being to the businessman. As a businessman, the owner manager has employees, customers, contracts, and unions to deal with. The human being has a wife, children, a mother, a father-in-law, assorted relatives, and, a dog, perhaps, all of whom are involved with him in one way or another. But the two, the human being and the businessman, are interrelated. They cannot be separated. And the wife must understand this and come to realize the multiple values in which she is involved.

The owner manager must begin sharing with his wife some of the meaning of what he has spent his life doing. This will not be easy . . . he has spent too many years protecting her from the smoke of war, or convincing her that this hero she's married to is strong enough to take care of himself and her, too. To admit sometimes that he's scared or that it hurts, and that he needs her understanding and help, may be one of the hardest changes to make. Not because he doesn't love her or doesn't want her to know about his business, but, mostly, because he is inarticulate and he doesn't know how to explain to others the way he feels. He grunts or mumbles in order not to explain.

As the owner manager becomes more tired and more lonely and more afraid, he finds he doesn't have the drive he once had to reach his ultimate goal. He just wants the business to level out. He doesn't want to struggle for more; he wants to be sure he can keep what he already has. But if he thinks that, if he allows himself to rest at this point, the dream will cease to exist. The business becomes a profitable hobby, a selfish occupation, or both. And the dream for which this man has bet his life, will die because he is lonely, tired, scared, and running out of time.

This is why his wife should become involved. While she may not fully understand the business dream, she can understand what it means to her husband. All she has seen is that her husband is too often away from home, that he's tired, concerned, preoccupied, harassed.

Her solution is to get him out of it. Why endure? She doesn't need more material compensation. If she does not understand the dream enough to keep from submitting to this solution, she will become an accomplice in her husband's destruction of his dream. If she is to assist him, he must help her to understand why she cannot allow him to destroy in his weak moments all those things he has spent his life building.

But how is she supposed to understand if her whole relationship with her husband has been like that of a non-participative passenger in the airplane with respect to the pilot? She's the perpetual passenger, and she has no idea why her husband insists on being the pilot, unless he explains it to her. She also has no idea what he has to do to keep up his proficiency as a pilot, unless he tells her.

She would like to understand. She would like to help. But he never wanted her to tell him whether he was flying too high or too low . . . he was the pilot and the plane would go his way. The husband, as an owner manager, cannot share this mystique of running one's own business, unless the other party recognizes the difficulty involved and can share the exhilaration. He thinks his wife won't be able to understand any of this or what it means to him and so he doesn't tell her.

If you think the founder's wife has troubles understanding her husband, think how difficult it is for the young wife whose husband is the son. She really has trouble following the founder's "flight plan." In her role as the wife of the heir, oftentimes too much is expected of her with no thought ever being given to her need, as well, to understand.

Add a few daughters who are the wives of sons-in-law and it's not hard to see that no man is really going to succeed in a business if his wife doesn't understand and appreciate the pressures, needs and demands the business places upon him.

The owner manager has two bosses: The government and his wife. Both share in the losses. Both share in the profits. But only one shares in the dream, and only one of them makes it worthwhile to win. The only way that she can understand the dream is for him to take the time to tell her about it. The time which he has left to share this dream is already running out.

Before it is too late the owner manager must explain to his wife about his dream and his goals. She must understand them or he must amend them. And, if she is to help in the pursuit of this dream, he must, in turn, understand her, and her fears and concerns for him.

THE DREAM

The owner manager has a concept, an idea, a philosophy, a goal or a dream for his business. And everything he does after setting that dream has one purpose: to reach that dream. But this is the part of himself that the owner manager almost always fails to reveal to his wife. He never asks her to evaluate it, amend it, participate in it. Before it is too late, the business owner must expose his wife to the basic elements of his business dream such as:

1. The desire always to have meaningful work to do until the Lord calls him.

2. The desire to have his wife understand him completely— understand both his work, and the relationship between his dream, his work, and his hopes for his family. Deep down he wants her to understand all of the trade-offs he must make in order to insure the comfort and security of his loved ones.

3. The desire to leave something of his creation behind him.

4. The desire to have his sons (or daughters) accept his dream, and hopefully, take on the same concerns some day. He wants this heir to accept his occupation with honor; to believe in what he believes in; to accept its challenges; and to assume its responsibility.

The acceptance of this responsibility is especially important, because (1) it is through this transfer that the business dream is continued; and (2) it is essential that it happen. At some point in time the owner manager needs to have—and (if he is honest) wants to have—his burdens and responsibilities lightened.

He wants to be admired and respected when he has reached the end of his useful life, and he desperately needs, at this crucial period, to have the time and the support to do all the things necessary to insure the sharing of this dream. But all too often, our dreams dissolve in time, until it's too late, and then all that remains is a desperate—and almost always badly executed—search to find a successor to keep the business going. I run across this fact all too often.

I'm asked too often to counsel a son whose father has taught him nothing but suspicion. Now the son can't command the respect and commitment of his own peers, and the father wants to know how he can find new heirs because his own have denied him.

I'm asked too often to consult with the man whose wife has lost the desire to become part of the dream—the man whose wife in her rejection has turned to the bottle; the owner manager who finally admits at age 60 that he won the wrong war. Like Midas, his golden touch has in the end destroyed the ones he loved.

I'm asked too often to consult with a man's wife and explain to her why in order to transfer his dream, an owner manager needs a wife and a mother, not a bookkeeper/wife or office manager. The owner manager can really find these talents in others. His wife's true vocation is to help build, fulfill, and share his dreams . . . to be what these others can never be.

I'm asked too often to counsel men whose advisors have done nothing in the years past other than prey upon their fears, whose suppliers look upon them as nothing more than a temporary outlet for their goods, and whose advisors have relegated them simply to the role of meal ticket.

And then people ask me why I contend that this man—the business owner manager—is so truly alone. Is it any wonder?

Just as wars are much too important to be left to generals, business dreams are too important to be left to those who don't care about them. Businessmen's dreams are much too important not to be shared with those who care, and the secret of success is to transfer these dreams to those who understand our needs, and for whom we care and feel responsible and with whom our business dreams are made, our family, suppliers, employees and friends.

As a start in helping his wife understand his business, the owner should have her meet and know his business team not on a professional basis at a board meeting or with the accounting firm while they audit the books, but on a relaxed, semi-personal level. This doesn't mean an owner manager must parade a long line of professional people through his dining room every week of the year—his managers, directors, bankers, accountants, consultants. It does mean, however, that the owner manager should be interested enough in the continuity of his business to take the pains to have his wife become acquainted with those he thinks deserving of the title "manager," "advisor" and "director." At the death of her husband these people should not be total strangers to her. Of course, it should go without saying that the vital prerequisite to making this relationship successful is for the owner manager to choose them wisely and carefully. It won't help his widow if they are incompetent.

WHO CARES WHAT THE BUSINESS IS WORTH

Although few men like to contemplate their own demise, it would save anguish not only for their widows but also for many other interested parties, if they took an active interest in planning for the disposition of their business and their estates while they are still alive, for passing along what they own and what they have built. There are many people, inside and outside the family, who are vitally concerned with the business owner's enterprise and the plans he has made for it. The IRS, his wife, his partner(s), his children, his employees, his customers, his suppliers, his executors, his potential investors and buyers all have an interest in the business and its worth. What is the nature of these interests?

1. *The IRS* has a definite voice in the worth of a company. It has long ago taken a position of interest in the earnings generated, and the owner has paid it a yearly dividend. However, the IRS is going to say, after the funeral, that its "partnership" interest must be satisfied before anyone else's. The whole world of taxes and estate planning is based upon this inevitable and irrevocable fact. I have yet to meet a man who willingly accepts as valid the IRS appraisal. Most owner managers say the IRS simply doesn't understand.

2. What about wives, sons and daughters, sons-in-law, brothers, sisters; in a word *the family*? Each, as an inheritor, gives a different value to a company, has a different view of it. Does this value or this view, include a guaranteed job, fringe benefits, a guarantee against risk, a privileged capital structure? Has the owner used stock ownership as a whip or bait, punishment or reward to his heirs? Is his company a family cow just meant to give its milk to the kids? Is it a license for privilege? Or is it a bastion for entrepreneurial

independence and self-fulfillment unequaled in economic society? Daughters who marry outside the business, and sons who inherit their jobs along with the rewards, never seem to agree on value.

What does all this do to the widow? She is an odds-on favorite to inherit the mess an owner leaves. Where does she go to get honest appraisal of value, helpful advice that treats her whole problem? Too often, what the business is worth to her is heartache, grief, too much responsibility, and a knock-down, drag-out family fight that no one wins.

3. Business "Partners"—a man's *co-investors*, so to speak, be they brothers, cousins, or "the other family," have a right to know an owner's plans. This is no place for secrecy. What are an owner's plans for his children? They have a right to know. Do survivors win everything and dispossess the heirs of the dead, or does the survivor have the responsibility to protect his "partner's" heirs? How long? Under what conditions? If there was ever a place for a business Solomon, this is the place. Books have been written on the oppression and expulsion of minority interests. Where does "control" lie after death?

Division of the shareholdings among the multiple heirs of a "business partner" creates a new set of "heirs," some in the business, some out. The wisdom of a Solomon is needed at times to pursue the best course.

4. *Employees*, too, have affixed a value to the company. Are their jobs guaranteed? Do they think so? Does the owner think so? Does the business supply status, security, and satisfaction for a working lifetime? Is the business a worthy vessel to contain *their dreams*? They know it's not worth a damn if the place closes up. Business values, like health, are oftentimes a reflection of a man's state of mind. Needing to sell is like being pregnant and unmarried. There isn't much time to find either a husband or an acceptable offer. The value that's put on a business when it has to be sold is probably the lowest it's ever going to be.

5. What's the company worth to the *executor* of the estate if he doesn't know how to run it, and he would probably like to get rid of it? Any trustee of closely held stock would bail out of the company because, without dividends, who wants the stock? Trustee responsibility for minority shareholders is an even tougher job.

6. What's a business worth to a *liquidator* in a forced sale? How many cents on a dollar? Is it about what he can sell it for on the block? Remember a quick turnover is the important way to leverage his investment.

7. Each *business owner* should ask himself at what price he honestly thinks he could sell his business to others, assuming that anybody would want it? The worth of his assets in a sale is far different from their worth to him as the manipulator and beneficiary of their profit-producing potential in combination with his labor. If he were the buyer, would his shares be as valuable as when he tried to sell them?

How does he value *reputation, integrity, market position*? Who puts the value on them? Independent appraisers too often feel value is only a physical asset, to be replaced if possible. Assuming the owner knows better, has he made sure this "value" will be preserved? Why is it that sellers always call this act "merging" and the buyers call it "acquiring?" Could this have something to do with the way they look at the business, even if it doesn't appear that way?

8. Suppose a business owner wanted to sell a share of his business to a *minority investor*. What is the investor buying? A return on investment, a job, preferential treatment, employment for his family? What is a *controlling interest* worth? What is a minority interest worth? As the man said, "Fifty-one percent of my business might be worth money, because it can get me elected president but 49% ain't worth nothing." How many family businesses actually pay dividends? How can a business owner expect controlling interests and minority interests to agree on anything when the spoils are one-sided and everybody feels "entitled"?

How can an owner establish a value that accommodates all these things and at the same time satisfies him? Can he really say "My company is worth X dollars?" An owner manager's opinion of his company's value is usually unrealistic or unacceptable. Of course, no two businessmen representing different interests will ever put the same value on anything. Each has different hopes and goals, limitations, restrictions, and demands. Each one also has different motivations and different reasons for wrapping up "business" in a finite value.

So it seems foolhardy that so little concern is given to one outstanding fact: namely, that very few family businesses are worth as much when the owner is dead as when the owner is alive. The owner manager, by his personal competence, judgment, skill, hard work and risk, does great things with those assets under his control. Remove him from the scene and the machinery doesn't work quite as it used to. Who takes over when he's gone?

Irrespective of the beneficiary—his heirs or a stranger—the maximum value he can set occurs when he leaves behind him a managment that can manage even better than he did. A man can take a lifetime to build up his worth. His widow and successors can see it disappear in a moment, if he did not plan for its perpetuation.

SETTLE ESTATE PLANS WHILE OPTIONS EXIST

It may be a chilling thought, but a good means by which the business owner can test whether or not his estate is in proper shape, is for him to pretend that he will die tomorrow, and then go over his estate plans with the proper advisors. With them he should examine such questions as: "Will my business survive? Am I unnecessarily making Uncle Sam one of my heirs? Do I have enough cash on hand to pay all the taxes? Where does that cash come from? Will my assets be distributed in a manner according to my wishes? Who will own and profit from my business? Will my wife have enough income? Who will control management of my company? Is there a clear and apparent successor ready to take over the business? Will my family and advisors be prepared to handle the business crisis immediately following my demise? "Advisors who specialize in estate planning should then assist him in putting his estate in order. Good estate planners will help the owner to look dispassionately and objectively at his present state of affairs, his business, his assets, his personal and corporate objectives. They will then assist him in determining exactly what problems may stand between him and the realization of his objectives. Finally, they should come up with a reservoir of possible solutions to these estate problems. Estate analysis is not a patent medicine guaranteed to cure all ills and difficulties. It will not add one jot to a man's personal assets except to point out how resources which might otherwise needlessly be lost can be conserved.

Estate planning is not a substitute for a lawyer or accountants. It is not a gimmick to save taxes, although tax saving is often one of the results of good estate planning. It is not a substitute for life insurance or any other form of capital. Most important, estate planning is not a short-cut to the owner manager's goals, and it is not a substitute for good, sound business judgment. Estate planning can do just one thing: it can enable a business owner to make intelligent decisions in matters of critical important to the people who mean the most to him—his family, his successors, and his managers.

Estate analysis is no job for amateurs. It is not a do-it-yourself kit for avoiding probate. This is no place for self-taught techniques. Estate planning starts with an analysis of matters as they exist. A list of assets and liabilities is compiled. The terms of the will are checked, and, if a current will does not exist, one is drawn up. Then life insurance should be checked and the owner's objectives put in writing. These should include personal goals as well as business planning. A search should be made of any contracts which could shift the owner's assets, not only at the time of his death but also at the time of his wife's death. Many essential phases of the estate planning process are governed by highly technical legal rules and considerations. That is why at the very minimum such a plan should involve the assistance of a lawyer, a C.L.U. and a competent bank trust officer. The result of this process will be a hypothetical probate of the owner's estate and a written plan for the succession of the business.

One of the disciplines the owner manager should impose on himself as part of the total task of estate planning is reviewing his will with his lawyer. It is incredible how many men die with wills which are, for all practical purposes, ancient history. They have legal documents drawn up at the inception of their business career (if they have them drawn up at all), and then let them gather dust in some safety deposit box. Men change through the years; their dreams, goals, and wishes change. In most cases, where the business owner has drawn up a will, the will is not changed one iota from the day it is written.

The man who does not have a will has decided that the state legislature is competent to determine who is to receive his estate and in what proportion. The man who has a will which leaves everything to his wife with no further instructions for the disposal of his estate has decided that his wife is qualified to manage his business and the investment of his funds. He has also decided that the Treasury Department should take money which otherwise would be available to his children.

Estate planning is not only intended for the distribution of one's assets after one's death; it is also intended to be used for the continuation and renaissance of the business after the planner is gone. It is not enough that the husband has shared his dreams and plans with his wife. He needs to provide her with legal documents to assist her in carrying out these plans. She has a right to know what to expect her role to be and what her husband intends that others' roles should be, and what business valuation she has to work with in fulfilling her obligations. There are a number of firms which specialize in establishing stock values. This kind of service need not be expensive, but it can be invaluable for a widow, if it has been performed prior to the death of the business owner. She will find the burden much easier to assume, if he has provided for a successor and prepared written instructions for the use of his estate and the continuity of the business.

The immediate burden of the widow is two-pronged. On the one hand she assumes the responsibility for the continuation of the business, unless her husband has installed his successor prior to his death. She, also, must settle the affairs with the government and attend to other legal, accounting and cash problems. Even if there were no tax laws to contend with, no problems associated with the cost of dying, the widow would still be faced with an overwhelming responsibility, that of running the business. It is very, very seldom that the unprepared wife successfully takes over the business after her husband is gone.

Therefore, a viable, solid plan for the continuation of the family owned business is essential. Without it, too often the only solution for widows is to sell the business. Unfortunately this is the very worst time to try to do so. The value of the business is depressed at the time of the owner's death, and the employees are demoralized.

It would be far better for all concerned, if the business owner took the responsibility for choosing and installing his successor within his lifetime and for making the arrangements for the use of his assets after his death. The arrangements must be made in the context of several important considerations:

1. Arrangements must be realistic and valid in view of current economic position and family situation. They should take into account proper legal and administrative mechanics. They should be known to those charged with carrying them out. There should be adequate provision for payment of taxes; Uncle Sam won't take inventories.

2   In making his decisions, the owner manager must use facts which were known to all of his advisors. He should have informed these advisors of all of the problems facing him at the time of his planning. The owner himself, must be aware of the consequences which flow from alternatives he has provided. He must inform his beneficiaries of their responsibilities under the provisions he has made.

3. Extensive practical experience in the settlement of estates indicates several major areas in which problems occur. The owner manager should think these through with his advisors in order to avoid them. They are excessive administration costs; inability of the estate to meet cash requirements; assets awarded to the wrong person; income problems after probate; no practical plan for the continuation of the business with tested leadership.

When all of the advisors to the business participate in the planning of the estate, both the owner and the beneficiaries profit, and the advisors can derive great satisfaction from their respective contributions. The board of directors and family members should also be included in this planning. Estate planning is, after all, a plan for the creation, utilization, and conversion of the resources of a business to implement the business owner's dream.

Chapter Eleven

Managing Time

In His wisdom, God gives to each of us a limited, finite number of hours in which to achieve our goals, both material and spiritual. He gives us these hours in sequence, day by day, month by month. If they are wasted, however, they are neither repeatable nor refundable. He gives the same amount to the rich and to the poor, to the young and to the old. Whatever successes we may achieve in this life will come from the purpose to which we put God's priceless gift—time.

Consider what God does with one day. He makes a day and takes out one-third for maintenance of the machinery, so to speak. He then gives us back two-thirds of that day. Look at that, if you will, as a model for your own use of the remaining time. How much time do you put back into the business to keep it working efficiently? You can't continually take out without putting in. It's like fresh air, or energy, or any other resource.

Fresh air used to be considered something we had in abundance. Now, fresh air is a matter of concern, as is the use of energy and other natural resources. Now, the cost of fresh air and fresh water is being charged into the cost of doing business. The quality of life is such that we cannot debase our world by unreasonable desire for short term profitability.

Cannot the entrepreneur be accused of overstating his annual profits if he is not allocating a fair proportion of his *time* as well as his other resources to doing all the things required to make his business a continuing successful operation? If he doesn't, when he goes, everything else goes with him.

WHERE SHOULD THE PRESIDENT PUT HIS TIME?

Since the major function of the president is to plan for the growth and successful continuity of his company, he cannot forever function as its hardest working tradesman. A working lifetime is less than 500 months. Everytime we take off one of those monthly watchband calendars and throw it away, we are throwing away an increasing percent of what is left. That realization is sobering. Time is not recallable. No warranties, no inventory, no quality assurance, no return of the deposit. Time just runs out.

I am concerned with time as our most finite and irreplaceable resource. Not, mind you, as an efficiency expert, but in a more philosophic sense. I look at time as the fuel for the vehicle which gives our lives purpose and meaning.

Two examples: (a) The ultimate justification for *health care* is that without it we can't lead a meaningful life and therefore, short of hypochondria, we justify taking care of ourselves because we need the physical strength to do those things we mean to do. (b) The ultimate justification for *profit* in our free enterprise system, again, short of economic hypochondria, is that it provides the vehicle for the continuity of the system and a vehicle for attaining social good by providing meaningful work. By the same token, I feel that the proper use of our *time* receives its justification from its purpose.

Our young people today have taught us a great deal about preserving what we have and not despoiling it by misuse or overuse. They've made the word "ecology" a household word. They have taught us that we are completely dependent upon a finite, material quantity of things called "the earth" and we have a responsibility to this finite resource.

The same is true with time. Under 21, when someone asks the young how old they are they always claim to be older, so they can drink booze or be admitted to the casinos in Las Vegas. But along about 45 or 50, we begin counting time from the other end. And it is then that we realize how finite a commodity it is and that we must have concern for its investment and use.

We begin to realize that all the things we can do and all the benefits we hope to accrue—physical, material and spiritual—are a result of the investment of time. Without such a conscious investment, we are not going to realize those things which we want to accomplish. And what we do with our lives is ultimately a judgment on how we have made use of that resource of time.

I've long felt that time must be purposeful. It can't just be efficient—e.g., read in the tub, watch T.V. while you eat, and all that sort of stuff. (I've been in one bad automobile accident already, trying to dictate some notes on my tape recorder and not seeing the car in front of me stop.) So, I am not going to ask you to do two things at once, but rather that our time should be apportioned— rationed, if you will—to assure the achievement of our goals.

How the owner-president manages this commodity called "time" has a determining effect upon the future of his business. If he sees his tenure as infinite, he will not prepare himself to train those who must carry on his dream into the new world. If he sees time as a compilation of experience rather than a series of new worlds, he will fail to keep pace with change and his company will not remain relevant in a changing world.

I belong to a very positive school. I believe we can do almost anything we want, and the price we pay for our goals is time. Tell me how you spend your time and I'll understand what your dream is and how well you are preparing to protect it, enlarge it, and preserve it for the future.

Do you consciously spend time in the preservation of your health so that the rock on which you base your talents doesn't all of a sudden roll out from under you? Do you spend meaningful time with your family? They are our real wealth. Or are these hours your reservoirs? When you need more time elsewhere how often do you seem to take it from the family? But it is not an infinite reservoir you can tap indefinitely anymore than you can tap the reservoir of sleep. You need both of these—family and sleep—to revitalize and reconstitute you for the work you hope to do.

One of the sobering things about an hourglass is that whenever you look at it, time always seems to be half gone. What about our own business hourglass? How much time do we figure there is left? How are we using it? Perhaps, what we really need is a schedule for the allocation of our time, just as we maintain a diet for the proper distribution of our food input.

Figuring a 50 or 60 hour week and allowing for a few vacations, the owner-manager works between 2000 and 3000 hours a year. How much of this total time should be allocated for maximum effectiveness in the development of himself, his business family, and his company? Try this "diet supplement" and your economic well-being is sure to improve—you won't be too thin from overwork, nor too fat from overconfidence. For example:

If 1% = 20-30 hours = 4-6 old fashioned ½ days — then why not plan:

- 1% — for half-day meetings with your directors — 4 times a year

- 1% — for half-day meetings with your advisors — 4 times a year

- 1% — for half-day meetings with your successor-management team — 4 times a year

- 1% — for a family evening with different directors/advisors/ managers — once a month

- 1% — for self-improvement seminars—once or twice a year.

In securing the future of your family-owned business, review how you spend your time and where you put your priorities. Unless you consciously use the hours given to you in preparing others to effect and adapt to change; unless you consciously plan the time to prepare yourself to turn over the reins to the heirs you have selected and helped to train, you are not keeping faith with your dream.

Ultimately, we must all take our joy and our glory and our sense of accomplishment from the abilities of those whom we have taught to share our dream—and whom we have prepared to carry it on. This is the final achievement of the family-owned business and the reason why it can weather storm and adversity. In its perpetuity lies the true immortality of the founder. And to assure it, we must commit our time, as we do to all other forms of well-being.

Chapter Twelve

Conclusion:
Planning for the Future

I stated very early in this book that the business owner who has not made plans for the continuity of his business is overstating his profits for when he goes, everything goes with him. I asked the reader to join me in the business owner's world and look at his problems, his pressures, his priorities, his myths, his alternatives, and his prospects for change. We have examined some of the steps which a business owner might take to help meet his needs and make the necessary changes.

In a broad sense, we have developed a "composite case" describing the nature of the family-owned business, its central characters, the roots of its difficulties, the basis for its opportunities, and its possibilities for adaptation and change. I believe the family-owned business has a bright future—that it's continuation as a social force is necessary to the growth and success of our country—and that its problems are capable of solution given the understanding and the commitment of those who believe in it and care about it.

The specific needs for change will vary within each individual business. Only the business owner, his family, his managers, his advisors, and his directors can supply the particular and specific facts necessary to permit each business to make the decisions necessary to assure its adaptability and continuation into the future. Therefore, having written on these pages the composite "case" out of the many thousands of family businesses I have been privileged to know, I ask *you* to write *your* own individual "case"—*your* book about *your* business. Do it on paper, not in your head. State the facts realistically and write them clearly so that you can't hedge. Admit alternative opinions, and don't forget to weigh all the important considerations and opinions. Involve all the people who have an investment in the future of your business in this exercise in order to provide their encouragement, information, organization, direction, and evaluation to the complete statement of the "facts" of your "case." Their help and commitment is vital to your success . . . and the keystone to your future planning.

A.   A CHECK LIST FOR BUSINESS OWNERS
    BEGIN AT THE BEGINNING

1.   *When* did you start/join your business? What was your background?

2.   *Why* did you start/join your business? Be honest with yourself.

3.   *Who* was with you when you started? What were their backgrounds?

4.   *What* was your early market/product/service concept?

5.   *What* were your assets—Financial, Technical and Managerial?

B.   BRING IT UP TO DATE

6.   *Who* is with you *now*, and when did they join you? What happened to the others?

7.   *What* has happened in the intervening years to you? to your family? to your company? to your employees? to your advisors? to your directors? to the product/service you

produce? to the market/customers you serve? Be honest and be complete. Make a chronological "history" of events; put dates on each occurrence.

a) *Draw* your organization chart realistically as it grew from:

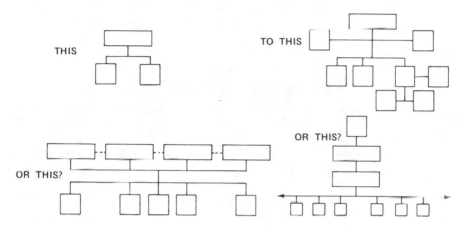

Be sure to include your directors/advisors/co-investors/family.

b) *Plot* your growth over the years in

1. $ annual volume
2. total employees
3. profit margins
4. personal income

c) *Relate* it to the FUTURE

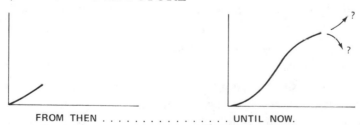

FROM THEN . . . . UNTIL NOW.

8. *What steps* have you taken to assure the continued success of your business?

9. *What plans* have you made for your estate, and the disposition of family interests in the family business?

10. *Who* is going to carry on your business when you leave it?

11. *What* is the order of priority . . . for you, personally . . . for the company?

12. *How much time* do you have left in which to take these necessary steps? What is influencing your time table?

13. *Who* is going *to help* you make these decisions and solve these problems? Are they with you, now? If not, when do you intend to find them? Are they aware of your concern? Are they equally committed to your goals? How do you attract their participation?

14. *What changes* must be made in the current operation of your business in the next year? Five years? 100 months?

15. *On whom* does *the burden* of action rest for making these changes? What are the options such person(s) may have in taking action? Which are the best courses of action? For you? For others? Why? In what priority? Are they in conflict?

16. *What further questions* do you find still need to be answered? How do you go about finding the answers?

17. *What plans* have you made for *your renaissance*, and the renaissance of your company?

If you have the courage to make this kind of commitment to your business . . . by facing the "facts," by articulating your concern and your hopes, by writing and studying your own "case" in the company of others who care, then there can be no doubt in my mind that we, you and I, share a common faith in the future of the family-owned business.

Instead of becoming the victims of change, we have committed ourselves to become its masters by planning for crisis, designing for continued relevancy, and surrounding ourselves with competent people who can help us assess, understand, and adapt to change. We have decided that our business has value beyond our lifetime, and we are preparing it to survive whatever winds of change may buffet it.

The owner manager who takes this kind of time, with his successor, his family, his employees, his advisors, and his directors to plan for the future of his business can view his inevitable withdrawal with equanimity and satisfaction. He can look back with pleasure upon a life well spent, and enjoy in his leisure years the feeling of pride which will come from watching a chosen successor guide with confidence and skill the company which he built with his own sweat, and guts, and dreams.

 # TWELVE COMMANDMENTS
for the
BUSINESS OWNER

1. Thou Shalt Share Thy Dream With Thy Family.

2. Thou Shalt Inform Thy Managers and Employees, "This Company Will Continue Forever."

3. Thou Shalt Develop a Workable Organization and Make It Visible on a Chart.

4. Thou Shalt Continue to Improve Thy Management Knowledge, That of Thy Managers and That of Thy Family.

5. Thou Shalt Institute an Orthodox Accounting System and Make Available the Data Therefrom to Thy Managers, Advisors, and Directors.

6. Thou Shalt Develop a Council of Competent Advisors.

7. Thou Shalt Submit Thyself to the Review of a Board of Competent Outside Directors.

8. Thou Shalt Choose Thy Successor(s).

9. Thou Shalt Be Responsible That Thy Successor(s) be Well Taught.

10. Thou Shalt Retire and Install Thy Successor(s) With Thy Powers Within Thy Lifetime.

11. Thou Canst Not Take It With Thee — So Settle Thy Estate Plans — Now.

12. Thou Shalt Apportion Thy Time to See That These Commandments Be Kept.

LÉON A. DANCO, Ph.D.

Index

191

Books about Family Business
From The Center for Family Business

"INSIDE THE FAMILY BUSINESS" by Léon A. Danco, Ph.D.

...the nation's recognized authority on privately held business draws on two decades of experience "inside" thousands of successful family-owned companies to write about the real keys to success: the attitudes, experiences, and relationships among the most important people in any family company...**the family members themselves.** In his well-known frank and concrete style, Dr. Danco explores the questions which arise . . . or should arise . . . at each stage in the growth of a family business, the mistakes that are commonly made, and **how they can be minimized or overcome.**

"BEYOND SURVIVAL: A Guide for the Business Owner and his Family" by Léon A. Danco, Ph.D.

. . . for the owner-manager of a successful family business — for the entrepreneur who made it and now wants, somehow, to ensure his dream survives beyond him. In this internationally acclaimed book, Dr. Danco draws **an honest and understanding picture of the business owner and his world:** the who's who of power, how to manage people and money, how to gain commitment from outside advisors, how to manage succession, and how to manage estate planning.

"OUTSIDE DIRECTORS IN THE FAMILY OWNED BUSINESS: Why, When, Who, and How" by Léon A. Danco.

. . . about working boards of outside directors, and about the family businesses they serve. This book goes point by point through **a concept that has been working effectively in thousands of privately held businesses for more than 20 years.** It is an easy to read, step by step manual for business owners who are concerned with providing a proven way to help assure growth and continuity in their successful family-owned businesses. This is a book about how to change existing boards, how to find and use working outside directors, how to organize and run worthwhile meetings, and about how to live happily with outside directors.

"FROM THE OTHER SIDE OF THE BED: A Woman Looks at Life in the Family Business" by Katy Danco.

. . . a book written by, for, and about women in family businesses — wives, ex-wives, wives-to-be, widows, daughters, daughters-in-law, sisters, sisters-in-law, cousins, and owners. Katy Danco, with the help and wisdom of the many women she has met over the past 20 years, has written **a book that helps to answer the important and difficult questions faced by the women who inhabit the fascinating, troublesome world of the successful family business.** Without answers to these and many other questions, it's likely that a family in business just won't succeed.

The Center for Family Business
P.O. Box 24268
Cleveland, Ohio 44124
216/442-0800